A SELF EXERCISE

MW01715095

to accompany

Eighth Edition

YOUR ATTITUDE IS SHOWING

A Primer of Human Relations

Elwood N. Chapman

Prentice Hall, Inc.
Englewood Cliffs, NJ 07632

Printed in the United States of America
10 9 8 7 6 5 4 3 2

ISBN 0-13-442476-X

Prentice-Hall International (UK) Limited, *London*
Prentice-Hall of Australia Pty. Limited, *Sydney*
Prentice-Hall Canada Inc., *Toronto*
Prentice-Hall Hispanoamericana, S.A., *Mexico*
Prentice-Hall of India Private Limited, *New Delhi*
Prentice-Hall of Japan, Inc., *Tokyo*
Simon & Schuster Asia Pte. Ltd., *Singapore*
Editora Prentice-Hall do Brasil, Ltda., *Rio de Janeiro*

TO THE INSTRUCTOR

This self-paced activity manual is designed to supplement the popular text YOUR ATTITUDE IS SHOWING. It is not intended that this guide stand alone as an instructional book. It's purpose is to enhance the learning of human relations skills. Students who complete material in the guide immediately after reading each chapter will keep the ideas longer. Application helps them to weave skills into their behavioral patterns. Their grades improve.

Of course, each instructor can use the guide to satisfy his or her own learning goals:

- INSTRUCTORS WHO ONLY HAVE LIMITED CLASSROOM TIME WITH THEIR STUDENTS CAN USE THIS GUIDE FOR ASSIGNMENT AND CONTROL PURPOSES—COMPLETING THE GUIDE WILL HELP COMPENSATE FOR LESS GROUP DISCUSSION.
- WORK EXPERIENCE INSTRUCTORS CAN USE THIS MANUAL AS A WAY TO STANDARDIZE WHAT STUDENTS CAN AND SHOULD LEARN ON THE JOB—STUDENTS CAN RETURN THE COMPLETED MANUAL AT THE END OF THE TERM FOR GRADING PURPOSES.
- SOME ORGANIZATIONS CAN USE BOTH THE TEXT AND THIS GUIDE IN COMBO AS A DO-IT-YOURSELF OR CORRESPONDENCE COURSE. EXCELLENT REPORTS HAVE BEEN RECEIVED WHEN USED IN THIS MANNER.
- THE EXTRA CASES (NOT FOUND IN TEXT) CAN BE USED FOR CLASSROOM DISCUSSION, EXTRA ASSIGNMENTS, OR FOR ORAL PRESENTATIONS.
- INSPIRATIONAL MESSAGES HAVE BEEN ADDED TO GIVE THE MANUAL MORE SUBSTANCE AND ZEST. THESE MESSAGES, ALONG WITH VARIOUS QUOTATIONS, ARE EXCELLENT FOR CLASSROOM DISCUSSIONS BUT HAVE BEEN ADDED PRIMARILY FOR STUDENTS WHO COMPLETE THE GUIDE WITH MINIMUM OR NO CLASSROOM INVOLVEMENT.

In all cases, completing the guide allows the student to proceed at her or his own pace. When classroom time is available for discussion purposes, completing the guide in advance gives the student more courage to participate.

'Education is learning what you didn't even know you didn't know."

Daniel J. Boorsten

TO THE STUDENT

Why should you make a contract with yourself to complete this guide in a conscientious manner? What personal benefits will you achieve for your time and effort? Results from field-testing indicate that the prospects for the following are excellent:

- YOU WILL INCREASE YOUR SELF-CONFIDENCE IN DEALING WITH ALL KINDS OF PEOPLE IN ALL KINDS OF SITUATIONS.
- YOU WILL START TO BUILD STRONGER AND MORE LASTING RELATIONSHIPS WITH CO-WORKERS AND FRIENDS.
- YOU WILL BE BETTER PREPARED TO REACH YOUR CAREER GOALS.

In a few cases, it will be suggested that you engage a supervisor or friend in an important exercise. Your willingness to do this will improve your human-relations skills and pave the way for you to have more meaningful relationships in the future.

GOOD LUCK!

Elwood N. Chapman

"Your mind is a sacred enclosure into which nothing harmful can enter except by your permission."

Arnold Bennett

CONTENTS

EXERCISES

A positive attitude is the most powerful and priceless personality characteristic one can possess.

The way to make the most of other physical and mental characteristics is to communicate them through a positive attitude.

INTRODUCTION

EACH CHAPTER IN THIS GUIDE CONTAINS FOUR SECTIONS.

1. **CHAPTER SUMMARY.** This short review of important chapter statements made in YOUR ATTITUDE IS SHOWING will help you make the transition from the text to this guide.

2. **RESPONSE TO CHAPTER HIGHLIGHTS.** This part gives you an opportunity to react to material in the text. Completing it in a conscientious manner will prepare you for examinations and help you complete the exercise that follows.

3. **EXERCISE.** This is the most important section in the chapter. The exercises will help you improve your competency in human relations, improve control over your personal attitude, and give you an opportunity to put what you have learned from the text into practice.

4. **CASES.** Special cases (not found in text) are spread throughout the guide. It is suggested that the student read each case carefully, form an answer either on paper or in his or her mind, and match with the suggested answers at the back of the manual.

5. **INSPIRATIONAL MESSAGES.** To make the guide more enjoyable students are encouraged to enjoy special thoughts (included in boxes) and various quotations.

6. **TEST YOURSELF.** Self-test questions (ten per chapter) enable you to check your comprehension and retention of the material covered in both the text and the guide. By answering these questions (and checking the correct answers in the back of the guide), you can measure your learning progress without instructor assistance. A final 100-question examination has been provided for your instructor. If you read the text carefully and complete this guide conscientiously, you should be able to achieve a high score in this examination.

HAVE FUN!

Having a charismatic personality (or even getting close)
is impossible without a positive attitude.

Chapter 1

YOU CAN'T ESCAPE HUMAN RELATIONS

CHAPTER SUMMARY

Most people drastically underestimate the importance of human relations.

There is much more to human relations than just getting people to like you.

Productivity should come first in any job, but human relations should never be neglected.

Negative employees put an added strain on their supervisor and co-workers.

RESPONSE TO CHAPTER HIGHLIGHTS

The first level of human relations can be described as:

____

The second level of human relations can be described as:

____

List two reasons why human relations should run a close second to productivity for an individual to enjoy career success.

1. ____

____

2. ____

____

Explain how an employee can have very high personal productivity and still not make his or her best contribution to a department.

____

____

____

____

Exercise 1 **CAREERS AND HUMAN RELATIONS**

Some careers require more human-relations skills than do others. For example, an airline flight attendant must be more competent in dealing with people than a mechanic.

This exercise will help you evaluate the importance of human relations in diversified careers. Please list three of your career goals in the spaces provided at the bottom of the exercise before you begin. Then rate (by a checkmark under the appropriate column) the relative importance of human relations in each career, including your own. When you have finished, you will be able to evaluate the importance of human relations in your career choices as compared to others.

CAREERS	CRITICALLY IMPORTANT	MOST IMPORTANT	IMPORTANT	UNIMPORTANT
Computer operator	______	______	______	______
Office manager	______	______	______	______
Flight attendant	______	______	______	______
Waitress	______	______	______	______
Bank manager	______	______	______	______
Policeperson	______	______	______	______
Salesperson	______	______	______	______
Laboratory technician	______	______	______	______
Research scientist	______	______	______	______
Bank Teller	______	______	______	______
Nurse	______	______	______	______
Librarian	______	______	______	______
Security guard	______	______	______	______
Telephone operator	______	______	______	______
Secretary	______	______	______	______
Mail carrier	______	______	______	______
Teacher	______	______	______	______
Politician	______	______	______	______
Your choices:				
____________	______	______	______	______
____________	______	______	______	______
____________	______	______	______	______

INSIGHT

A positive attitude costs nothing but gives much. It enriches those who receive, without making poorer those who give. It takes but a moment, but the memory of it sometimes lasts forever. None is so rich or mighty that he can get along without it, and none is so poor but that he can be made rich by it. It can be your most priceless possession.

TEST YOURSELF

For each statement below, put a check under true or false.

TRUE	FALSE		
_____	_____	1.	To achieve career success an individual should place human relations first and productivity second.
_____	_____	2.	An individual who doesn't want to become skillful at human relations can easily find a career in which it is unimportant.
_____	_____	3.	Human relations competencies can be learned.
_____	_____	4.	There is a positive correlation between high competency in human relations and career success.
_____	_____	5.	Human relations, among other things, is devising a strategy that will give you the breaks at the expense of others.
_____	_____	6.	A negative employee can have the same effect as a spoiled apple in a barrel.
_____	_____	7.	A positive employee ads to a team spirit by bonding everyone together in a more enthusiastic mood.
_____	_____	8.	An employee with poor human-relations skills can hurt the efficiency of a department even though his personal productivity is very high.
_____	_____	9.	A quick look at the text Your Attitude Is Showing will show that the primary human relations competencies are listed inside of the front and back covers.
_____	_____	10.	Human relations plays a far more important role in career success than most people will admit.

Turn to the back of the book to check your answers.

TOTAL CORRECT _________

"ANOTHER DAY AT SCHOOL. . ."

Chapter 2

HUMAN RELATIONS CAN MAKE OR BREAK YOU

CHAPTER SUMMARY

Developing human-relations skills often makes the big difference between career success and failure.

A high degree of self-confidence is necessary to achieve human-relations competency.

There is a symbiotic relationship between attitude and personality.

There appears to be little correlation between high mental ability and the ability to work well with people.

RESPONSE TO CHAPTER HIGHLIGHTS

Explain why a very quiet person might have human-relations problems.

____

____

List three reasons why human relations is more important today than it was thirty to forty years ago.

1. ____

____

2. ____

____

3. ____

____

Give one reason why highly verbal, extroverted people are sometimes poor at human relations.

____

____

____

____

Exercise 2 **SELF-CONFIDENCE INVENTORY**

This self-evaluation exercise is designed to help you measure your personal confidence in initiating communications with others, which, in turn, can lead to the building of better human relationships. Circle the number that indicates where you fall in the scale from 1 to 10. After you have finished, total your scores in the space provided.

I am completely at ease when it comes to speaking up in class or in other groups.	10 9 8 7 6 5 4 3 2 1	I never take the initiative to speak up in groups of any kind.
When I have all the facts, I do not hesitate to present my opinion.	10 9 8 7 6 5 4 3 2 1	I never present my opinion even though I know I am right.
I enjoy initiating a conversation with a stranger if there is no danger involved.	10 9 8 7 6 5 4 3 2 1	Even under ideal (safe) conditions, I would never talk to a stranger.
It doesn't bother me at all to join informal groups already involved in communications.	10 9 8 7 6 5 4 3 2 1	I would feel so awkward I would never join an informal group of any kind without an invitation.
If a co-worker and I had a personality conflict, I would initiate a meeting to reconcile our differ ences.	10 9 8 7 6 5 4 3 2 1	If a co-worker and I had a personality conflict, I would let time solve it.
I would have complete confidence to approach my supervisor on any matter important to me.	10 9 8 7 6 5 4 3 2 1	I would never approach my supervisor under any circumstances.
I would quickly volunteer to speak over a microphone at a dinner meeting.	10 9 8 7 6 5 4 3 2 1	Under no conditions would I volunteer to speak in front of any group.
I enjoy walking into strange social environments when I do not know anyone.	10 9 8 7 6 5 4 3 2 1	I refuse to walk into strange social environments even if I know I will meet a friend.

In conversations, I always look people in the eye.	10 9 8 7 6 5 4 3 2 1	I never look anybody in the eye.
I have more than enough self-assurance to initiate a relationship with anyone.	10 9 8 7 6 5 4 3 2 1	My self-assurance is zero when it comes to initiating relationships with others.

TOTAL SCORE ________

If your point total is 50 or above, you are doing your part or more in building relationships. If your score is under 50 points, more initiative on your part might be desirable. The field-testing of this exercise showed that most people should strive for more self-confidence in building relationships with others.

CASE STUDY • THE TAKER

Everyone in the office likes Maureen. She is warm-hearted, and full of intriguing stories about her active social life. Maureen is seldom absent, never late, and remains positive and upbeat throughout her work day.

But Maureen does not carry her full share of the workload. She often seeks help when she gets behind in her work but she never pays back the people who help her. On top of this, her skills are not up to standard and there is no indication she intends to make improvements. One co-worker expresses her attitude toward Maureen in this way: "Sure, she's got personality that won't stop, but I think she is taking advantage of the company's stated policy that they won't terminate anyone unless there is a major violation of some kind. We are letting her get by on her charms while the rest of us carry the big part of the load."

Should Maureen's manager take action? If so, what form should it take?

Please turn to page 92 for author's comments.

TEST YOURSELF

For each statement below, put a check under true or false.

TRUE	FALSE		
____	____	1.	Employers often hire applicants as much on their attitudes as their job skills.
____	____	2.	A major personality change is necessary if one is to become skillful at human relations.
____	____	3.	It is necessary to become an extrovert to become good at human relations.
____	____	4.	The magic of a positive attitude is that it has a way of making your eyes sparkle and your smile more engaging.
____	____	5.	This guide will do nothing to help you get a new job, but it will help you after you get it.
____	____	6.	A positive attitude will not give you a better self-image.
____	____	7.	It is better not to approach co-workers at all than to feel clumsy about doing it.
____	____	8.	Field-testing of the Self-Confidence Exercise showed that most people need more self-confidence.
____	____	9.	Silence in an individual can often be interpreted as aloofness.
____	____	10.	There is an extremely high correlation between high mental ability and human-relations competency.

Turn to the back of the book to check your answers.

TOTAL CORRECT ________

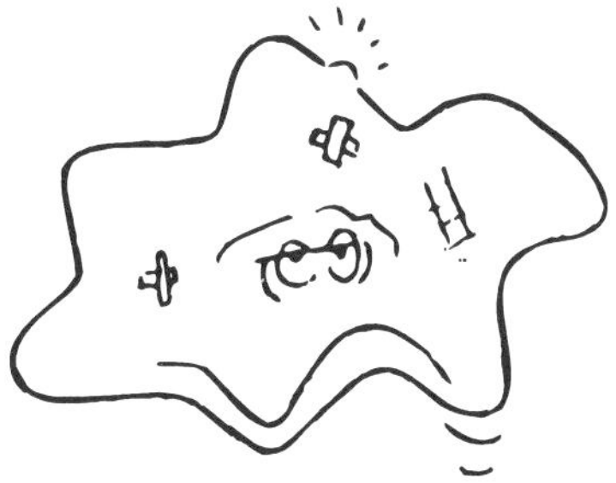

ONE OF THOSE DAYS!

Chapter 3

HOLD ON TO YOUR POSITIVE ATTITUDE

CHAPTER SUMMARY

Your attitude speaks so loudly I can't hear what you have to say.

The moment you can no longer be positive regarding your job, your chances for success diminish.

People who can push unpleasant (negative) factors out of their minds and dwell on positive things are usually more successful.

If you are not careful, people with negative attitudes can ruin your positive one; on the other hand, if you remain positive, you can sometimes bring others to the "positive side."

RESPONSE TO CHAPTER HIGHLIGHTS

Please name the three forms of communication.

1. ____________________

2. ____________________

3. ____________________

In a larger sense, attitude is the way you look at

____

A positive attitude is essential to career success for many reasons. Name three:

1. ____________________

2. ____________________

3. ____________________

List three methods for keeping your attitude positive on a day to day basis.

1. ____________________

2. ____________________

3. ____________________

Exercise 3 **KEEPING A POSITIVE JOB ATTITUDE**

All jobs or careers have both plus and minus factors. The more an employee concentrates on the positive factors, the more positive the attitude of the individual is apt to be.

This exercise will help you separate the positive from the negative in your present job or one you have had in the past. Listed below are twenty different factors that employees respond to in either a positive or negative manner. You are asked to place P in front of each factor you are positive about and N in front of each factor you are negative about. Please add other important factors about your job in the blanks provided, and rate those as well.

_____ Job permits you to go to school
_____ Salary
_____ Fringe benefits
_____ Physical working environment
_____ Promotional possibilities
_____ Quality of leadership in management
_____ Quality of your immediate supervisor
_____ Amount of personal freedom
_____ Opportunity to dress as you please
_____ Transportation and commuting distance
_____ Good company cafeteria

Other: ______________________________
____
____

_____ Working hours are ideal
_____ Compatible co-workers
_____ Good or bad parking facilities
_____ Learning opportunities
_____ Recognition from management
_____ Good internal communications
_____ Job permits you to live where you please
_____ You are doing what you want to do
_____ Equipment is modern
_____ Good heating and air conditioning
_____ Regular breaks

____
____
____

_____ TOTAL POSITIVE FACTORS

_____ TOTAL NEGATIVE FACTORS

If you counted more positive than negative factors (and they are equally or more important to you), then by concentrating on them, you should become even more positive about your job. You will be less concerned with negative factors and talk about them less. This change will have a good influence on your attitude.

If, however, you counted more negative than positive factors, you have three choices: (1) Convert some negative factors to positive. (Perhaps you made a mistake in these ratings.) (2) Uncover some positive factors you previously ignored. (3) Seek a new work environment where more positive factors exist.

TEST YOURSELF

For each statement below, put a check under true or false.

TRUE	FALSE		
______	______	1.	Attitudes are caught, not taught.
______	______	2.	A positive attitude is a consistent smile.
______	______	3.	There is no relationship between attitude and the number of friendships one enjoys.
______	______	4.	Attitudes are carried from one environment (job) to another environment (personal life).
______	______	5.	To be a positive person, you need not think your company is perfect.
______	______	6.	The more an individual concentrates on the positive factors in life, the more positive he or she will be.
______	______	7.	People who can list more negative job factors than positive ones should quit their jobs immediately.
______	______	8.	People who are totally negative about their jobs, and remain so for an extended period of time, should find a new job.
______	______	9.	Attitude can be defined as the way you look at things mentally.
______	______	10.	Serendipity is an attitude that is appreciated by others.

Turn to the back of the book to check your answers.

TOTAL CORRECT ________

"DON'T ASK ME . . . I JUST WORK HERE."

Chapter 4

WHEN PEOPLE STEP ON YOUR ATTITUDE

CHAPTER SUMMARY

Anticipate that people will now and then step on your attitude. Sometimes lightly. Sometimes heavily.

"Bouncing back" quickly requires understanding, determination, and some special techniques.

Occasionally firm, confrontational action on your part may be necessary.

RESPONSE TO CHAPTER HIGHLIGHTS

List three out of the four "bounce back" strategies suggested in the chapter.

1. ______________________________

____

____

2. ______________________________

____

____

3. ______________________________

____

____

The last time somebody stepped on my attitude was:

____

____

____

Exercise 4 **BOUNCE BACK EXERCISE**

Assume an authority figure of some kind (supervisor, teacher, parent, etc.) has stepped on your attitude so hard that you are emotionally upset. Which of the following action steps would you consider to restore your positive attitude in the shortest period of time? Place a checkmark in the square of the three suggestions you like best.

- ☐ Play it "cool" and allow time to restore your positive attitude.
- ☐ Have a serious talk with yourself in which you convincingly explain why your positive attitude is too valuable to allow any authority figure to "steal" it from you.
- ☐ Make an appointment to openly discuss the matter with the authority figure who stepped on your positive attitude.
- ☐ Sulk.
- ☐ Figure out a way to retaliate so you can, in effect, step on the authority figure's attitude.
- ☐ Forgive and forget and above all refuse to take being stepped on personally.
- ☐ Position yourself where it won't happen again.
- ☐ Tell yourself you are too "big" a person to allow such a little thing to get under your skin.
- ☐ Seek counseling and guidance from a professional.

TEST YOURSELF

For each statement below, put a check under true or false.

TRUE	FALSE		
____	____	1.	When someone steps on your positive attitude it is like stepping on your ego.
____	____	2.	People who work for a living normally get their attitudes stepped on a few times each day.
____	____	3.	The best way to keep insensitive co-workers from stepping on your attitude is to ignore them.
____	____	4.	Sometimes a boss can come down on your attitude so hard it is impossible to bounce back.
____	____	5.	It is a mistake to nurse a deflated attitude.
____	____	6.	When your ego is deeply hurt is can take months to bounce back to your previously positive attitude.
____	____	7.	The longer you allow your attitude to be depressed the more difficult it is to bounce back.
____	____	8.	The more you value your positive attitude the more willing you will be to employ "bounce back" techniques and strategies.
____	____	9.	It is a good idea to apologize when you inadvertently step on another person's attitude.
____	____	10.	If someone steps hard on your positive attitude and you allow it to turn you negative for a long time you have, in effect, permitted this person to "steal" your positive attitude.

Turn to the back of the book to check your answers.

TOTAL CORRECT ________

Chapter 5

VERTICAL AND HORIZONTAL WORKING RELATIONSHIPS

CHAPTER SUMMARY

A relationship is a <u>feeling thing</u> that exists between two people who associate with each other.

You cannot consistently work with or near people or communicate with them frequently without having working relationships with them.

Good relationships must be built.

Horizontal working relationships exist between co-workers; vertical working relationships exist between a worker and a supervisor.

RESPONSE TO CHAPTER HIGHLIGHTS

The lifeblood of a good relationship is

____

In building good working relationships there are two things to avoid:

1. ____

2. ____

Explain, in your own words, why improving horizontal relationships can also improve a vertical one.

____

____

____

"Joys shared are doubled; sorrows shared are halved."
ANON

Exercise 5 PRIORITIZING YOUR WORKING RELATIONSHIPS

> "This turned out to be a profitable exercise for me because I discovered I had been neglecting a few key relationships that were influencing my personal progress."
>
> Telephone Company Employee

If you are not currently employed, you need not complete this exercise.

Although all of your job relationships are important, some may be more critical to your career success than others. This exercise will help you decide whether you have been underestimating and neglecting some relationships in favor of others.

Please list from five to ten important relationships you have in your present job in the spaces below—listing what you feel to be your most important relationship first and so on down the line. After analyzing the list, underline the names of those whom you feel you have neglected in recent weeks.

1. 2.

3. 4.

5. 6.

7. 8.

9. 10.

All working relationships are important. The individual who concentrates on building relationships with a few at the expense of others is demonstrating insensitivity and damaging his or her career.

CASE STUDY • THE LONER

Gloria Grace is an outstanding equipment specialist. She can operate any machine in the office, and her language skills are flawless. She consistently produces more than anyone else. As a result, she is given extra assignments, which she completes in record time. This, of course, takes pressure off the other staff members.

But Mrs. Grace is not really a part of the office team. She talks to her coworkers only when absolutely necessary. When she finishes her own work, she reads or writes letters. She never pitches in to help others when they are behind schedule. Mrs. Grace apparently does not need or want human contact. She never leaves her work stations except to go to the rest room or to the company cafeteria, where she eats alone. She seems to love machines and books. Not people.

If you were her office manager, would you leave Mrs. Grace alone or try to get her to be part of the team? Why?

To compare your thoughts with those of the author, please turn to page 92.

TEST YOURSELF

For each statement below, put a check under true or false.

TRUE FALSE

______ ______ 1. Two people cannot meet regularly on the job or work in the same general area without having a relationship.

______ ______ 2. If you don't want a relationship with a co-worker, the best thing to do is to ignore this individual.

______ ______ 3. We tend to see ourselves as others see us.

______ ______ 4. Most good relationships usually come about automatically.

______ ______ 5. The lifeblood of a good relationship is two-way communication.

______ ______ 6. The primary responsibility for creating and maintaining a strong vertical relationship rests with the worker.

______ ______ 7. Supervisors are in charge of creating and maintaining good horizontal working relationships.

______ ______ 8. The purpose of prioritizing working relationships is to discover those being neglected.

______ ______ 9. Personal relationships (as opposed to family and working relationships) are the only ones in which an individual has free choice.

______ ______ 10. There is an extremely high correlation between high mental ability and human-relations competency.

Turn to the back of the book to check your answers.

TOTAL CORRECT ________

"I'VE HEARD ALL THAT OLD STUFF BEFORE."

Chapter 6

PRODUCTIVITY— A CLOSER LOOK

CHAPTER SUMMARY

Management is primarily interested in human relationships because of productivity.

The productivity of both individuals and departments is measured and monitored.

People seldom reach their potentials; that is, there is a gap between what they could do and what they actually do.

It is possible for an employee to increase his or her personal productivity but decrease departmental productivity because of poor human-relations skills.

RESPONSE TO CHAPTER HIGHLIGHTS

Place a check next to the job in which productivity is most easily measured.

________ Assembly-line worker ________ Secretary

Identify the three parts in the diagram below.

1. ______________________

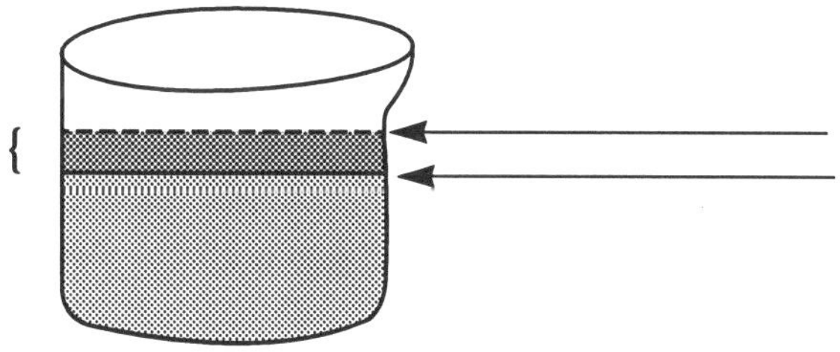

2.
3.

An individual's potential is made up of the following characteristics:

1. ______________________________ 2. ______________________________

3. ______________________________ 4. ______________________________

5. ______________________________

"The person who rests on his laurels is wearing them in the wrong place."

Anon

Exercise 6 **JOB IMPROVEMENTS THAT WOULD MOTIVATE ME**

Some job improvements motivate employees more than others. Other improvements seem to provide little or no motivation to do a better job. What about you? Please assume you are occupying a job that is not highly motivating to you and management makes the following improvements. Place a check in the appropriate column opposite each improvement.

IMPROVEMENTS	(1) WOULD MOTIVATE ME ON A SUSTAINING BASIS	(2) WOULD MOTIVATE ME ON A TEMPORARY BASIS	(3) WOULD NOT MOTIVATE ME
1. Higher pay	_____	_____	_____
2. Better relationships with co-workers	_____	_____	_____
3. Better retirement plan	_____	_____	_____
4. Better relationship with my supervisor	_____	_____	_____
5. More job security	_____	_____	_____
6. Receiving more recognition	_____	_____	_____
7. Less distance to travel to work	_____	_____	_____
8. Being accepted more by others, including those in my department	_____	_____	_____
9. Improved lighting, better restrooms, and air conditioning	_____	_____	_____
10. Being told more often how I am doing by my supervisor or others	_____	_____	_____
11. Improved health program paid for by employer	_____	_____	_____
12. Feeling more relaxed to have some fun on the job	_____	_____	_____
13. Having a better cafeteria with lower prices	_____	_____	_____
14. Opportunity to communicate more with management	_____	_____	_____
15. Better equipment to use	_____	_____	_____
16. Being involved more in management decisions	_____	_____	_____
17. Better hours to work	_____	_____	_____

	(1)	(2)	(3)
18. Being treated with more dignity	_____	_____	_____
19. Moving to a better building in a better location	_____	_____	_____
20. Being trusted more; less supervision	_____	_____	_____

You were not told in advance that the odd-numbered statements deal with physical changes, while the even-numbered ones deal with psychological or human-relations changes. Would you like to find out which classification motivates you the most?

If so, add the checkmarks found in columns one and two opposite the odd-numbered improvements and place the total on the line for physical changes. After doing this, go through the identical process for the even-numbered improvements and write the total on the other line.

TOTAL SCORE FOR ODD-NUMBERED (PHYSICAL) IMPROVEMENTS _____

TOTAL SCORE FOR EVEN-NUMBERED PSYCHOLOGICAL IMPROVEMENTS _____

If you have a larger score in the physical box than in the psychological box, it would appear that physical improvements motivate you the most. If the opposite is true, it would appear that psychological improvements are more motivating to you.

This interesting comparison could be valuable should you become a supervisor in the future. As a supervisor, the more you can motivate people, the more successful you will be. Yet you may have little control over physical matters. (Your superiors may not approve the increase in salary you recommend for one of your employees.) But you do have control over psychological matters. If you can't give a high-producing employee an immediate raise, at least you can provide recognition or psychological support.

Field-testing of this exercise showed that psychological improvements are more motivating to the majority of people. This is often a signal that maintaining good relationships with people is extremely important to these individuals. What about you?

INSIGHT

Most of us must learn to live in a comfortable way with our many inherited traits and characteristics. We can make improvements through better grooming, health programs, and even plastic surgery. But after doing our best in these areas, we must recognize that further improvement must come through better communication of what we already possess. The vehicle that will accomplish this is a positive attitude.

TEST YOURSELF

For each statement below, put a check under true or false.

TRUE	FALSE		
_____	_____	1.	Physical improvements (such as air conditioning) motivate employees more than psychological improvements (such as recognition).
_____	_____	2.	Few improvements in job conditions motivate workers on a sustaining basis.
_____	_____	3.	Supervisors have more control over psychological than physical improvements.
_____	_____	4.	It is easy to measure the productivity of a secretary.
_____	_____	5.	Most people reach their full potential regularly.
_____	_____	6.	Potential and mental ability are one and the same.
_____	_____	7.	The primary responsibility of a supervisor is to help a worker achieve his or her maximum productivity.
_____	_____	8.	Employees in a department are interdependent as far as departmental productivity is concerned.
_____	_____	9.	The difference between what a worker is doing and what he or she could do under ideal conditions is called the "productivity gap."
_____	_____	10.	There appears to be little or not correlation between high productivity and good human relations in a department.

Turn to the back of the book to check your answers.

TOTAL CORRECT _________

"YES SIR, I UNDERSTAND THE NEW POLICY PERFECTLY."

Chapter 7

THE WINNING COMBINATION

CHAPTER SUMMARY

Happy employees are usually—but not always—high producers.

The most important factor management seeks is the right combination of personal productivity and human relations.

An increase in personal productivity should be accompanied by increased attention to horizontal relationships.

You don't have to be miles ahead of others for management to recognize you.

RESPONSE TO CHAPTER HIGHLIGHTS

Name the two different ways you can increase your personal productivity above that of your co-workers.

1. ____________________

2. ____________________

In increasing one's personal productivity, what are the advantages to paying increased attention to horizontal working relationships with co-workers?

1. ____________________

2. ____________________

3. ____________________

Name the four primary factors that management seeks in employees.

1. ____________________

2. ____________________

3. ____________________

4. ____________________

Explain why an employee who does not have customer contact can still benefit from a good service attitude.

____

____

____

Exercise 7 WORK CHARACTERISTICS YOU SEEK IN AN EMPLOYEE (Supervisor's Copy)

As part of a course in Human Relations your employee ______________________________ has studied the ten factors below and rated them as to their importance.

Attitude	Personal productivity
Human-relations skills	Willingness to assume responsibility
Assertiveness	Creativity (submitting new ideas)
Reliability	Attention to details
Job accuracy	Follow through

You are requested to rate these characteristics independently so that the employee can compare your priorities with his or her own. We feel this comparison can be a rewarding growth experience for the employee. Would you, therefore, please list the ten factors on the pyramid below? Place the factor you believe to be the most important at the top, the least important at the bottom. Please list all ten factors.

1. ______________________________
2. ______________________________
3. ______________________________
4. ______________________________
5. ______________________________
6. ______________________________
7. ______________________________
8. ______________________________
9. ______________________________
10. ______________________________

Now please compare your own ratings with the ratings chosen by your employee. Where your priorities are different, it would be most helpful to discuss why. Through this exercise, the employee may become even more valuable to the total productivity of your department.

Your cooperation is sincerely appreciated.

Exercise 7 WORK CHARACTERISTICS YOU SEEK IN AN EMPLOYEE (Employee's Copy)

If you are not currently employed, please have a fellow student, friend, or relative act as your supervisor.

This project will enable you to discover those work characteristics your immediate supervisor appreciates the most. This, in turn, will help you satisfy him or her better and improve your career progress. There are two steps involved: (a) You are to complete the material found on this page. (2) Independently, your supervisor (or a replacement) is to complete the material on page 24.

Please study the ten job factors listed below.

Attitude	Personal productivity
Human-relations skills	Willingness to assume responsibility
Assertiveness	Creativity (submitting new ideas)
Reliability	Attention to details
Job accuracy	Follow through

Most supervisors consider these factors to be vital to job success; in fact, many claim that these are the factors most managers seek in the employees they wish to promote. After you have studied them carefully, place them in the pyramid below in the order of importance to you. The factor you feel to be least important should be placed on the bottom. All ten factors must be listed.

1. ______
2. ______
3. ______
4. ______
5. ______
6. ______
7. ______
8. ______
9. ______
10. ______

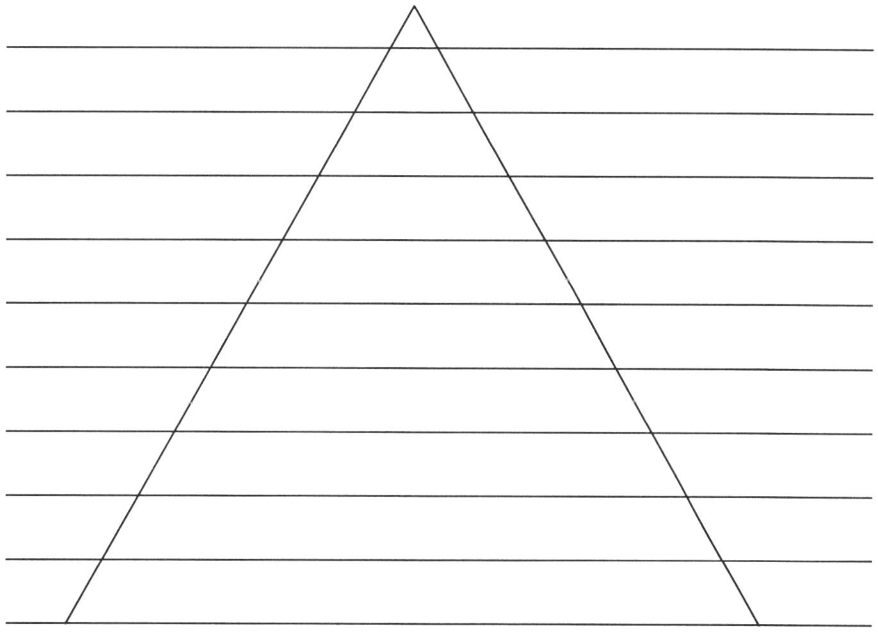

The next step is to take the duplicate exercise (page 24) to your immediate supervisor so that he or she can rate these characteristics independently before you sit down and discuss the results.

Field-testing demonstrated that supervisors are most cooperative in participating in this exercise.

TEST YOURSELF

For each statement below, put a check under true or false.

TRUE	FALSE		
_____	_____	1.	Supervisors always tell you the personal characteristics they appreciate most.
_____	_____	2.	An increase in personal productivity should be accompanied by increased attention to horizontal relationships.
_____	_____	3.	The kind of employee management seeks is one who is willing to produce at the level of others.
_____	_____	4.	Organizations prefer employees who are satisfied with their personal potential.
_____	_____	5.	The exercise in this chapter is designed primarily to help you build a better relationship with your immediate supervisor.
_____	_____	6.	Most employees know the work characteristics their supervisors seek.
_____	_____	7.	Management seeks a 40/60 blend in employees—40% productivity and 60% human relations.
_____	_____	8.	Happy employees are automatically top producers.
_____	_____	9.	Productivity ultimately includes the quality of service provided the customer.
_____	_____	10.	A machinist in a factory does not need a service attitude.

Turn to the back of the book to check your answers.

TOTAL CORRECT _________

"I'M NEVER ANXIOUS TO LEAVE WORK EARLY."

Chapter 8

YOUR MOST IMPORTANT WORKING RELATIONSHIP

CHAPTER SUMMARY

The most important working relationship you must deal with is the one between you and your immediate supervisor.

A supervisor should be a teacher, counselor, and leader; but you may never have a supervisor who lives close to your expectations.

Every supervisor must create and maintain a discipline line—which is never easy to do.

Learning how to build and maintain a strong, warm, open, and productive relationship with your supervisor is a challenge. Your future career may depend upon how well you are doing it.

RESPONSE TO CHAPTER HIGHLIGHTS

The chapter lists ten tips that should help you build a better relationship with your supervisor. Please summarize them below.

1. ______________________________

2. ______________________________

3. ______________________________

4. ______________________________

5. ______________________________

6. ______________________________

7. ______________________________

8. ______________________________

9. ______________________________

10. ______________________________

"People seldom want to walk over you until you lie down."

ANON

Exercise 8 **SELF-ASSESSMENT**

Your most important and delicate working relationship is the one between you and your immediate supervisor. This exercise is designed to help you evaluate and improve this vital relationship through the process of self-assessment. When you evaluate the relationship in private without any communication with your supervisor, you will need to be honest about the contribution you have made and what improvements you might be willing to make in the future.

Please circle the number that indicates where you fall in the scale from 1 to 10 on the following factors:

I believe I have done everything possible to develop a sound relationship with my supervisor.	10	9	8	7	6	5	4	3	2	1	I admit I have done almost nothing to develop a sound relationship with my supervisor.
I have always taken advantage of opportunities to communicate with my supervisor.	10	9	8	7	6	5	4	3	2	1	I have been stubborn and have never taken advantage of opportunities to communicate.
I have been 100% fair with my supervisor.	10	9	8	7	6	5	4	3	2	1	I admit I have not been the least bit fair with my supervisor.
I keep my personal productivity as high as possible to improve my relationship with my supervisor.	10	9	8	7	6	5	4	3	2	1	I produce only as much as I must to keep my job.
To keep a better relationship with my supervisor, I do everything possible to keep good relationships with my co-workers.	10	9	8	7	6	5	4	3	2	1	I am not making any effort to keep good relationships with co-workers.
I have never bad-mouthed my supervisor.	10	9	8	7	6	5	4	3	2	1	I bad-mouth my supervisor every day both at work and at home.
I seldom nurse a small gripe that could hurt my relationship with my supervisor.	10	9	8	7	6	5	4	3	2	1	I am currently nursing a number of small gripes.

(Continue on next page)

I respect the need for a formal working relationship with my supervisor.	10 9 8 7 6 5 4 3 2 1	My supervisor is stuffy and unapproachable. I can't respect such authority.
I have earned the respect of my supervisor and have been aboveboard on all matters	10 9 8 7 6 5 4 3 2 1	I have taken advantage of every opportunity to undermine my supervisor.
I have given my supervisor every possible chance to build a good relationship with me.	10 9 8 7 6 5 4 3 2 1	I have never given my supervisor a chance to build a good relationship with me.

TOTAL SCORE ________

If you rated yourself 80 or above, you are obviously doing your part and more to build a good working relationship with your supervisor. If you rated yourself between 50 and 80, some improvement on your part might be called for. If you rated yourself under 50, you may not be doing your part.

Although your supervisor, as a manager, has the primary responsibility to build a good relationship with you, your own responsibility is considerable. If you do not go partway in building such a relationship—perhaps because of a personality difference of breakdown in communication—you are hurting your career progress.

"WHAT'S WRONG WITH THE OLD SYSTEM?"

INSIGHT

Nowhere is a positive attitude more appreciated than on-the-job. There are three reasons for this.

1. For many people, work is not what they prefer to be doing. Performing tasks next to a positive person makes what they are forced to do more enjoyable.
2. Some co-workers have extremely difficult private lives. The only place they find positive people is near their work stations.
3. Supervisors depend upon the positive attitudes of their employees to establish a "team spirit." Your positive attitude makes his or her job easier.

TEST YOURSELF

For each statement below, put a check under true or false.

TRUE	FALSE		
____	____	1.	Employees who do not go partway in building a good relationship with their supervisors hurt their career progress.
____	____	2.	An employee is 70 percent responsible for building a good relationship with his or her boss.
____	____	3.	Supervisors establish working climates primarily through the use of discipline lines.
____	____	4.	A discipline line is an imaginary point beyond which the employee senses she or he should not pass lest some form of disapproval and possible disciplinary action take place.
____	____	5.	Theory X represents a structured, controlling leadership style.
____	____	6.	Theory Y is a participative, more permissive leadership style.
____	____	7.	There is no evidence that employees transfer negative attitudes toward other authority figures to their supervisors.
____	____	8.	The easiest and the quickest way to destroy your relationship with your supervisor is to go over the supervisor's head on a problem that involves the department.
____	____	9.	It is a good policy to make a buddy out of your supervisor.
____	____	10.	Discussing your supervisor in a negative way with co-workers is often considered to be unethical.

Turn to the back of the book to check your answers.

TOTAL CORRECT ________

INSIGHT

A person not considered beautiful by physical standards, can still be regarded as "beautiful" with a cheerful, positive outlook.

A positive attitude can provide higher energy levels, greater creativity, and an improved personality.

Chapter 9

UNDERSTANDING THE NATURE OF RELATIONSHIPS

CHAPTER SUMMARY

Work relationships have many characteristics, some of which can be isolated.

Understanding these characteristics can help one to create, maintain, and repair a relationship.

Youth is not a career handicap if the young employee can build good relationships with more mature co-workers and supervisors.

Most relationships will not last a long time unless the mutual regard theory is in operation.

RESPONSE TO CHAPTER HIGHLIGHTS

Please list and briefly explain the six relationship characteristics dealt with in the chapter.

1. ______________________________

____

2. ______________________________

____

3. ______________________________

____

4. ______________________________

____

5. ______________________________

____

6. ______________________________

____

Exercise 9 EVALUATING A PERSONAL RELATIONSHIP (OPTIONAL)

It is extremely difficult for two people to discuss and evaluate the relationship between them. There are many reasons why this is true. (1) It takes a high degree of personal confidence to initiate such a sensitive conversation. (2) It is difficult to evaluate the relationship without being over-critical about personalities. (3) Sensitive points from the past might surface. (4) Damage might occur if one or both persons take the result too personally.

With these points in mind, you are invited—on a purely optional basis—to participate in this exercise. Before you make your decision, consider the following data from field-testing of the exercise.

Thirty percent of those invited participated in the exercise.

All those participating rated it highly.

Most stated that their relationships improved as a result of the exercise. The statement "we learned to understand each other better" was common.

If your decision is yes, please select the other person carefully. Choose only a person with whom you already have a healthy relationship. Close friends, spouses, and children seem to work best. Also, select an individual who has the time and will take the evaluation procedure seriously.

Once the second person has agreed to participate, ask this individual to complete the form printed on the following page. While he or she is doing this, complete one yourself (they are identical). Then sit down and discuss the differences openly. Through the discussion, insights can be gained and improvements made.

OPTIONAL EXPERIMENT

"Appreciation is like an insurance policy—it needs to be renewed now and then."

ANON

RELATION EVALUATION FORM

(Using the scale of 1 to 10, circle the number that indicates the state of the factor under consideration.)

There is a high level of humor in this relationship.	10	9	8	7	6	5	4	3	2	1	This relationship needs more humor.
There is 100% two-way communication in this relationship.	10	9	8	7	6	5	4	3	2	1	There is almost no communication in this relationship.
There is a total absence of tension in this relationship.	10	9	8	7	6	5	4	3	2	1	There is considerable tension that needs to be eliminated.
There are no irritating mannerisms involved.	10	9	8	7	6	5	4	3	2	1	There are a number of irritating mannerisms that need to be discussed.
I feel free to go to this person to discuss mutual problems.	10	9	8	7	6	5	4	3	2	1	I cannot discuss mutual problems with this person.
The mutual reward theory (both parties going partway) works 100% in this relationship.	10	9	8	7	6	5	4	3	2	1	I feel I am doing far too much of the giving in this relationship.
There are no listening problems in this relationship—both parties listen.	10	9	8	7	6	5	4	3	2	1	There are some real listening problems in this relationship.
This relationship has shown substantial improvement recently.	10	9	8	7	6	5	4	3	2	1	This relationship has deteriorated recently.
There is no conflict because of age difference.	10	9	8	7	6	5	4	3	2	1	There is something of a generation gap.
All previous misunderstandings have been resolved.	10	9	8	7	6	5	4	3	2	1	There are still some misunderstandings to be resolved

TOTAL SCORE ________

RELATION EVALUATION FORM

(Using the scale of 1 to 10, circle the number that indicates the state of the factor under consideration.)

There is a high level of humor in this relationship.	10	9	8	7	6	5	4	3	2	1	This relationship needs more humor.
There is 100% two-way communication in this relationship.	10	9	8	7	6	5	4	3	2	1	There is almost no communication in this relationship.
There is a total absence of tension in this relationship.	10	9	8	7	6	5	4	3	2	1	There is considerable tension that needs to be eliminated.
There are no irritating mannerisms involved.	10	9	8	7	6	5	4	3	2	1	There are a number of irritating mannerisms that need to be discussed.
I feel free to go to this person to discuss mutual problems.	10	9	8	7	6	5	4	3	2	1	I cannot discuss mutual problems with this person.
The mutual reward theory (both parties going partway) works 100% in this relationship.	10	9	8	7	6	5	4	3	2	1	I feel I am doing far too much of the giving in this relationship.
There are no listening problems in this relationship—both parties listen.	10	9	8	7	6	5	4	3	2	1	There are some real listening problems in this relationship.
This relationship has shown substantial improvement recently.	10	9	8	7	6	5	4	3	2	1	This relationship has deteriorated recently.
There is no conflict because of age difference.	10	9	8	7	6	5	4	3	2	1	There is something of a generation gap.
All previous misunderstandings have been resolved.	10	9	8	7	6	5	4	3	2	1	There are still some misunderstandings to be resolved

TOTAL SCORE ________

"People are lonely because they build walls instead of bridges."

ANON

TEST YOURSELF

For each statement below, put a check under true or false.

TRUE	FALSE		
______	______	1.	As long as productivity is high, what a co-worker does in his or her private life should be of no concern to a supervisor.
______	______	2.	In a mutual-reward relationship, both parties come out ahead.
______	______	3.	Whether or not a habit or mannerism becomes an irritant depends upon the tolerance level of the other party.
______	______	4.	A basic human-relations principle is to respect and treat every person as a unique and special individual.
______	______	5.	The United States has become more a "mosaic" of different cultures than a "melting pot."
______	______	6.	There are certain dangers involved when it comes to dating people at work; one is when the supervisor dates someone in his or her department.
______	______	7.	The "hurt syndrome" often occurs when one person becomes over dependent upon another.
______	______	8.	Many relationship overtones exist without having any negative effect upon productivity.
______	______	9.	Every relationship needs to be built and maintained on an individual basis.
______	______	10.	The relationship between two people can often be better understood if isolated from the personalities that create it.

Turn to the back of the book to check your answers.

TOTAL CORRECT ________

"I ALWAYS ANSWER THE TELEPHONE PLEASANTLY."

Chapter 10

SUCCESS AS A TEAM PLAYER

CHAPTER SUMMARY

In some areas, a working "team" (circle) is replacing the traditional approach (pyramid) to supervision.

In team arrangements, employees are expected to go a long way in managing themselves.

Future teams and traditional departments will accommodate members from diverse cultures.

RESPONSE TO CHAPTER HIGHLIGHTS

Write out the four Cs that represent characteristics of an effective team member.

1. ______________________________

2. ______________________________

3. ______________________________

4. ______________________________

List five attitude factors that need to be present among members to make a team successful.

1. ______________________________

2. ______________________________

3. ______________________________

4. ______________________________

5. ______________________________

Exercise 10 ORIENTATION OF EMPLOYEE FROM FOREIGN CULTURE

You are a team leader with eight employees. The top management of your firm strongly supports the team approach and is anxious to employ qualified people from all cultures. Your team serves customers both in person and by telephone. Yesterday, one of your team members was appointed as a leader in another area. As a replacement, you have been assigned a Japanese woman who is new to this country. Her clerical skills are excellent but her use of the English language is weak. List the steps you would take to make sure she becomes a strong and respected team member within 90 days. Compare your suggestions to those at the bottom of the page.

1. ____

____

____

2. ____

____

____

3. ____

____

____

4. ____

____

____

5. ____

____

____

____

SUGGESTIONS

1. Introduce Japanese woman at special meeting where refreshments are served. Coach her ahead of time to give a short talk on her background and special skills.
2. Provide her with a weekly "sponsor" until she has worked closely with all seven members.
3. Meet with her on a daily basis to discuss any special problems she may be having.
4. Encourage her to take an "English as a second language course" whether or not she prepares to become a U.S. Citizen.
5. Review her progress in thirty days with other team members.

TEST YOURSELF

For each statement below, put a check under true or false.

TRUE	FALSE		
_____	_____	1.	Those who prefer the traditional approach to supervision feel that most employees prefer and require frequent and steady supervision to produce at their highest levels.
_____	_____	2.	Employees who like the team idea best enjoy managing others.
_____	_____	3.	It is more difficult to be a team member than a regular employee.
_____	_____	4.	Management is interested in establishing teams because they offer the promise of higher productivity.
_____	_____	5.	The more you identify with a new co-worker from a foreign culture the better.
_____	_____	6.	MRT is needed more to make a team work effectively than it is in a regular department.
_____	_____	7.	Those who have played team sports have insights that can give them an edge when it comes to being a member of a work team.
_____	_____	8.	Concentration is one of the four Cs.
_____	_____	9.	Skills learned by being a good team member do not help an individual who later joins a traditional department.
_____	_____	10.	The main reason management is converting departments into teams is to reduce expenses.

Turn to the back of the book to check your answers.

TOTAL CORRECT ________

Chapter 11

STRESS MANAGEMENT: RELEASING YOUR FRUSTRATIONS HARMLESSLY

CHAPTER SUMMARY

A frustration is the inner feeling of disturbance or anxiety you experience when you meet a temporary block to your immediate goal.

Sometimes when people become highly frustrated, they become aggressive and hurt their relationships with others.

A mature person is one who has learned to release his or her frustrations harmlessly.

RESPONSE TO CHAPTER HIGHLIGHTS

Below please list four ways in which you can put your understanding of the frustration-aggression hypothesis to work for you.

1. ______________________________

2. ______________________________

3. ______________________________

4. ______________________________

Give two reasons why it is counterproductive to direct one's aggressive behavior toward a large corporate structure.

1. ______________________________

2. ______________________________

Please list below three situations or problems that are often frustrating to you. Select those that may tempt you to lash back at others or cause you to injure relationships with co-workers or friends.

1. ______________________________

2. ______________________________

3. ______________________________

"You'll never lose your equilibrium by doing too many good turns."

ANON

Exercise 11 **CHOOSING APPROPRIATE WAYS TO RELEASE YOUR FRUSTRATIONS HARMLESSLY**

In this exercise you are to assume that your frustration-aggression level (threshold) has almost been reached and that you need a harmless way to let off steam. The idea is to release this steam without hurting or injuring your relationships with others. In short, you always have options. You can, at the point of release, select a harmless (rather than harmful) form of behavior.

On the following page you will find a list of possible things you might do at the "point of release" if you are at work. On the second page you will find a list of possible things you might do if you are at home or away from work. Please complete both forms.

Place a checkmark in column 1 if you feel the action would be dangerous. By doing this you automatically eliminate the possibilities in the other two columns. If you do not place a checkmark in column 1, then you should place one in column 2 to indicate that as far as you are concerned, the action is harmless; that is, it would not hurt relationships with others.

Next, please check column 3 if you feel the action described is appropriate for you. In other words, this action would be natural and comfortable for you to do.

IF YOU CHECK BOTH COLUMNS 2 AND 3, YOU APPEAR TO HAVE FOUND A SUITABLE AND HARMLESS WAY TO RELEASE AGGRESSIONS CAUSED BY FRUSTRATION.

EXERCISE

CASE STUDY • MR. OVERTIME

Mrs. Adams is a hard-working and capable employee. She considers herself fortunate to have found a job close to home with a firm that has an excellent salary schedule and fringe benefits. Because Mrs. Adams is a single parent of two, medical and dental benefits are especially important to her. And equally important is leaving work on time so that she can pick up her children before the daycare center closes.

All is not working out as well as she had anticipated. A fast starter herself, Mrs. Adams soon discovered that her manager is the opposite. Mr. Terry does not get around to handing out special assignments until early afternoon on most days. Then, he picks up speed and puts all such assignments into an emergency classification. His style causes her great frustration. Mrs. Adams could produce more in the morning but the extra afternoon assignments frequently force her to work late and impose on a friend to pick up her children.

What should Mrs. Adams do?

Match your answer with that of the author on page 92.

THINGS TO DO TO RELEASE YOUR AGGRESSIONS ON THE JOB

RELEASES	(1) HARMFUL TO HUMAN RELATIONS	(2) HARMLESS TO HUMAN RELATIONS	(3) APPROPRIATE FOR ME
Slam a door where it can be heard.	______	______	______
Slam a door where it cannot be heard.	______	______	______
Blow up in front of your supervisor.	______	______	______
Let off steam in front of a co-worker.	______	______	______
Count to ten under your breath.	______	______	______
Move around physically.	______	______	______
Take an unauthorized 30-minute break.	______	______	______
Go home sick.	______	______	______
Swear so others can hear.	______	______	______
Swear under your breath.	______	______	______
Steal some company property.	______	______	______
Make some personal phone calls.	______	______	______
Rave about the good old days to anyone who will listen.	______	______	______
Go to the bathroom.	______	______	______
Ask to see the company nurse.	______	______	______
Take an unauthorized coffee break.	______	______	______
Tell your supervisor you feel faint, then go lie down.	______	______	______
Write a letter on company time.	______	______	______
Go to the pub and have a drink.	______	______	______
Start cleaning out your desk or do some task you don't like.	______	______	______
Sulk silently where you are.	______	______	______
"Dream" about something pleasant.	______	______	______
Talk to yourself.	______	______	______
Sing to yourself.	______	______	______
Do a crossword puzzle.	______	______	______
Let off steam by talking to a co-worker who sometimes uses you for the same purpose.	______	______	______
Ask your supervisor for a raise.	______	______	______

Other ways:

________________________________	______	______	______
________________________________	______	______	______
________________________________	______	______	______

THINGS TO DO TO RELEASE YOUR AGGRESSIONS ON AT HOME

RELEASES	(1) HARMFUL TO HUMAN RELATIONS	(2) HARMLESS TO HUMAN RELATIONS	(3) APPROPRIATE FOR ME
Go jogging.	_____	_____	_____
Listen to some music.	_____	_____	_____
Turn the music up and scream.	_____	_____	_____
Swear a lot.	_____	_____	_____
Slam doors all through the house.	_____	_____	_____
Cook some exotic foods.	_____	_____	_____
Get drunk.	_____	_____	_____
Spill it out to a neighbor.	_____	_____	_____
Spill it out to a close friend.	_____	_____	_____
Yell at someone.	_____	_____	_____
Go bowling.	_____	_____	_____
Eat more than you should.	_____	_____	_____
Wash your hair.	_____	_____	_____
Throw rocks at the moon.	_____	_____	_____
Go shopping and buy some things you can't afford.	_____	_____	_____
Call someone long-distance and complain a lot.	_____	_____	_____
Work in your garden.	_____	_____	_____
Do something nice for another person.	_____	_____	_____
Throw a party.	_____	_____	_____
Take a long drive.	_____	_____	_____
See a friend who is a good listener and will understand.	_____	_____	_____
Read a good book.	_____	_____	_____
Get mad at yourself for getting frustrated in the first place.	_____	_____	_____
Take your dog for a walk.	_____	_____	_____
Play the piano.	_____	_____	_____
Take it out on a friend or a spouse.	_____	_____	_____

Other ways:

______________________________	_____	_____	_____
______________________________	_____	_____	_____
______________________________	_____	_____	_____

TEST YOURSELF

For each statement below, put a check under true or false.

TRUE	FALSE		
_____	_____	1.	Some people are successful in eliminating all frustrations in their lives.
_____	_____	2.	Frustration is the feeling of disturbance or anxiety you experience whenever a personal goal is interrupted.
_____	_____	3.	It is counterproductive to direct one's aggressive behavior toward an organization.
_____	_____	4.	It is more difficult to find harmless ways to release your frustrations (aggressions) on the job than it is at home.
_____	_____	5.	Self-victimization often occurs when you are mistreated by others.
_____	_____	6.	Understanding the frustration-aggression idea helps a person to avoid taking things personally.
_____	_____	7.	Verbal aggressive behavior usually does not harm human relationships.
_____	_____	8.	People who are perpetually frustrated often need to come up with alternate goals.
_____	_____	9.	Some people never seem to discover harmless ways to release their aggressions.
_____	_____	10.	Frustration thresholds fluctuate on a daily basis.

Turn to the back of the book to check your answers.

TOTAL CORRECT ________

"WHO'S FRUSTRATED?"

Chapter 12

RESTORING INJURED RELATIONSHIPS

CHAPTER SUMMARY

Reopening communication lines is the first step in the restoration of an injured relationship.

Leaving a damaged relationship line unrepaired—even if the injury was caused by the other party—can turn you into a victim and hurt your career progress.

The restoration of any relationship requires a degree of willingness to be accessible and listen to the other party.

RESPONSE TO CHAPTER HIGHLIGHTS

List three disadvantages to leaving a damaged relationship unrepaired.

1. ______________________________

2. ______________________________

3. ______________________________

Name three out of the four principles that can assist one in restoring a damaged relationship.

1. ______________________________

2. ______________________________

3. ______________________________

Out of the three rebuilding strategies, name your favorite and explain why.

____

____

____

"The art of being wise is the art of knowing what to overlook."

WILLIAM JAMES

Exercise 12 **BREAK THE ICE EXPRESSIONS**

In restoring a previously healthy relationship, taking the first step is the most difficult. Assume that you and a co-worker had a misunderstanding yesterday and you want to clear it up quickly regardless of who might be at fault. Listed below are some "break the ice expressions" that may lead to an open discussion that could, in turn, restore the relationship. Select the three you like best by placing a check in the appropriate box. After doing this, write out two expressions you prefer over those listed.

☐ "Look, Marge, you have my apology for what happened yesterday."

☐ "Hi, Harry. I just want you to know I am willing to forgive and forget the little incident yesterday. It really doesn't matter to me how or why it occurred."

☐ "Marge, our relationship is very important to me. I don't want what happened yesterday to come between us."

☐ "Harry, we've become a little irritable with each other recently. I think it is time we review our relationship. How about a cup of coffee?"

☐ "Our relationship isn't what it used to be, Harry. I think it is time to sit down and discuss the rewards we should be giving each other."

☐ "We've been rather testy with each other recently and yesterday things got out of hand. I'd like to take you to lunch and forget it. Okay?"

☐ ____

☐ ____

CASE STUDY • THE UNDISCIPLINED WORKER

Sara feels comfortable with Cassie, a warm-hearted young lady who works next to her in the word-processing center. Sara consistently helps Cassie with technical work problems; in return, Cassie does many nice things for Sara. Little gifts. Social introductions. Sara admits she would deeply miss her mutually rewarding relationship with Cassie.

But Sara can tell from the manager's attitude that Cassie is skating on thin ice as far as her job is concerned. Reason? Cassie has yet to learn that she must keep her personal and work life separate. Cassie's afterwork life-style is so hectic that she is emotionally and physically drained when she gets to work each morning. By the time she begins her first assignment on her word processor, it is time for the mid-morning break. Result? Despite Sara's attempts to cover up for her, Cassie's low productivity and frequent mistakes have come to the attention of the manager. Sara, seven years older and more experienced, knows that to survive in any job one must learn to regulate one's personal life so that there is enough energy left over for work. Sara knows this only too well: she once lost a job for the same reason. Sara finally decides that she must make this point clear to Cassie or Cassie will lose her job.

How should Sara go about doing this?

Compare with suggested answer from author on page 92.

TEST YOURSELF

For each statement below, put a check under true or false.

TRUE	FALSE		
_____	_____	1.	All human relationships occasionally become damaged.
_____	_____	2.	Fortunately, minor fall-outs between workers seldom hurt productivity.
_____	_____	3.	The longer an injured relationship is left alone the easier it is to repair.
_____	_____	4.	Emotional conflicts can be more stressful in the workplace than working overtime.
_____	_____	5.	Leaving a damaged relationship alone (even if caused by the other party) can turn you into a victim.
_____	_____	6.	Most damaged relationships are left unrepaired because neither party is willing to "break the ice" and initiate communications.
_____	_____	7.	Apologies are useless.
_____	_____	8.	Accepting a "little white lie" is not a good way to help another save face and restore a relationship.
_____	_____	9.	A discussion centered around MRT is a weak way to restore a severely damaged relationship.
_____	_____	10.	Some people would rather replace an important relationship than try to restore it.

Turn to the back of the book to check your answers.

TOTAL CORRECT _________

"SENIORITY COUNTS FOR SOMETHING."

Chapter 13

ATTITUDES AMONG CULTURALLY DIVERSIFIED CO-WORKERS

CHAPTER SUMMARY

Cultural diversification in the workplace is the wave of the future.

Cultural attitudes are mental sets either for or against those from cultures other than your own.

There are ways in which you can improve your attitude toward all co-workers and thereby increase your contribution to productivity.

RESPONSE TO CHAPTER HIGHLIGHTS

I rated myself a ________ on the Cultural Diversification Comfort Zone Scale.

List the three suggestions made by the author to improve the way in which you can build better relationships with all co-workers, especially those from cultures other than your own.

1. ____

____

2. ____

____

3. ____

____

Provide an example of how MRT might work between you and a new co-worker from a culture of your choice.

____

____

____

____

____

____

Exercise 13 **THE ORIENTATION OF MARY CHIN**

Assume that you are the supervisor or team leader of a group of high-tech employees in a science laboratory. A new employee, Mary Chin, has been assigned to your team and you wish to assist her in getting off to a good start so she can make her best possible contribution. You have had a preliminary interview with Ms. Chin and you find her to be quiet, intense, and fearful as to how she will be accepted by co-workers. Mary possesses many skills important to laboratory work.

Please list below three suggestions you would make to Mary prior to her first day in her new assignment.

1. ______________________________

2. ______________________________

3. ______________________________

As her supervisor, please list three suggestions you would make to members of your team to help Mary find the acceptance she will need.

1. ______________________________

2. ______________________________

3. ______________________________

ACCEPTABLE ANSWERS

Suggestions to Mary: 1. Provide names of team members and a few positive comments about each individual. 2. Give Mary a copy of her job description but stress her over-all responsibilities as a team member. 3. Take time to introduce Mary personally to each team member. 4. Assign a sponsor to give any special assistance to Mary that might be appropriate. 5. Take Mary to lunch so that she will feel comfortable with you as her superior.

Suggestions to team members: 1. Ask for a volunteer to act as a sponsor for the first thirty days. 2. Present a brief background on Mary's skills and a small amount of upbeat information on her background. 3. Mention the special contributions she can make to team productivity. 4. Give her ample time to make her adjustment. 5. Welcome any suggestions from team members on what you as her team leader might do during the first thirty days of her employment.

TEST YOURSELF

For each statement below, put a check under true or false.

TRUE	FALSE		
____	____	1.	A prejudice is, in effect, a mental set or attitude.
____	____	2.	Attitudes based upon out-dated prejudices are easily changed.
____	____	3.	It is often more rewarding to build a MRT relationship with a co-worker from another culture than it is from your own.
____	____	4.	Some employees unknowingly favor co-workers from their own culture.
____	____	5.	Your total contribution to your firm is a combination of what you produce yourself plus what you help co-workers produce.
____	____	6.	The sooner you rush in and build a strong relationship with a new employee the better.
____	____	7.	New employees from Pacific Rim countries are normally less intense concerning their work than those from other cultures.
____	____	8.	Above all else new employees need to know they are making a significant contribution.
____	____	9.	A new employee from a culture not already represented in a work team is often at a double disadvantage.
____	____	10.	Individuals from foreign cultures seldom become effective supervisors.

Turn to the back of the book to check your answers.

TOTAL CORRECT ________

Chapter 14

SUCCEEDING IN A NEW JOB OR ASSIGNMENT

CHAPTER SUMMARY

If you take these ten tips seriously, you will avoid many mistakes others make.

A friendly person is one who uses certain positive signals when she (or he) meets others. The more you send out, the more you receive back.

When you join an organization, you should carefully assess the grooming situation and decide what dress standards are best for you and your career.

Read all company material carefully; the more you learn about your new organization the better.

RESPONSE TO CHAPTER HIGHLIGHTS

Fill in the missing word in each of the following sentences.

1. Ask questions but learn to ask the ________________ ones.
2. Conserve your ________________ at the beginning.
3. Take a calendar ________________ to work with you.
4. Use good ________________ in working extra hours and taking your breaks.
5. Don't ________________ your education and intelligence.
6. Be ________________, but don't be an eager beaver.
7. Make friends, but don't make ________________ friends too soon.

INSIGHT

Some positive attitudes seem to "shine through" other personality characteristics and in the process the total image of the individual becomes brighter and more attractive to others.

Exercise 14 **BEHAVIORAL CHANGE COMMITMENTS**

Although you may have adjusted successfully to one or more previous jobs, this exercise is designed to help you make measurable improvements in the future. Many psychologists claim that the ideal time to make behavioral improvements is during a job or assignment change. One of many reasons for this is that you will probably be motivated to win the acceptance of your new co-workers.

The exercise on the next page will help you identify those specific areas in which you feel you need to make the greatest improvement. Here are three tips you are urged to follow.

1. Do not place a check in the first column unless you honestly intend to make a personal contract with yourself to show a measurable improvement. Limit yourself to no more than three commitments in this column.

2. Limit yourself to not more than five checks in the second column because it is better to concentrate on a few important changes than to spread yourself so thin that nothing happens.

3. Circle the one single check mark where you feel you need to make immediate improvement and you intend to start today.

Although the exercise is designed primarily to assist you in adjusting to a job switch, whether inside or outside your organization, you may decide to make some behavioral changes in your present situation. If you don't start making improvements now, you may forget your commitments to yourself before your next change in work environment occurs.

Please proceed with the exercise.

INSIGHT

Attitudes are caught, not taught. Most teachers are quick to admit that their attitudes are "picked up" by their students. We may transmit our negative attitudes on one wave length and our positive attitudes on another, but both seem to travel at the same speed and within the same perimeter. This principle sends us two signals. One, it is almost impossible to teach another (child, employee) to be positive. Two, setting a good attitude example is more important than we may have thought.

BEHAVIORAL CHANGE COMMITMENTS

POSSIBLE AREAS OF IMPROVEMENTS	(1) I HEREBY MAKE A PERSONAL CONTRACT WITH MYSELF TO IMPROVE SUBSTANTIALLY IN THESE AREAS	(2) I INTEND TO MAKE MORE EFFORT TO IMPROVE IN THESE AREAS	(3) NO IMPROVEMENT NEEDED
Learning more about the organization; reading more available materials	________	________	________
Sending out more positive, friendly signals	________	________	________
Doing a better job of building a good relationship with my supervisor	________	________	________
Learning to do a better job of asking the right questions at the right time	________	________	________
Making friends with all co-workers on an even basis; not showing favorites	________	________	________
Becoming more assertive without being aggressive or militant	________	________	________
Using a calendar notebook to improve my efficiency	________	________	________
Improving my reliability; not being absent or late to work	________	________	________
Setting a better productivity tempo; achieving a better balance between work and human relations	________	________	________
Refusing to bad-mouth others in the organization	________	________	________
Becoming a better listener	________	________	________
Having a more positive attitude	________	________	________
TOTAL	________	________	________

TEST YOURSELF

For each statement below, put a check under true or false.

TRUE	FALSE		
_____	_____	1.	When arriving at work it is a good idea to circulate around and make contact with co-workers before immersing yourself in your assignment.
_____	_____	2.	If you frequently report to work late, management will lose interest in your excuses.
_____	_____	3.	It is quite common for a new employee to catch a cold and miss a day or two of work during her (or his) first weeks of employment.
_____	_____	4.	Fear of being considered stupid is a prime reason why many new employees do not ask more questions even though it would be better if they did.
_____	_____	5.	Unauthorized overtime work and failure to take breaks can involve you and your employer in labor difficulties.
_____	_____	6.	Behavioral changes are more apt to happen during a job switch.
_____	_____	7.	It is discourteous to let your eyes wander when someone is talking to you in a private conversation.
_____	_____	8.	A person who creates a good first impression is one who confines himself to sending nonverbal signals.
_____	_____	9.	The main reason people do not send more signals is that they lack the confidence to send them.
_____	_____	10.	People don't care how much you know until they know how much you care.

Turn to the back of the book to check your answers.

TOTAL CORRECT _________

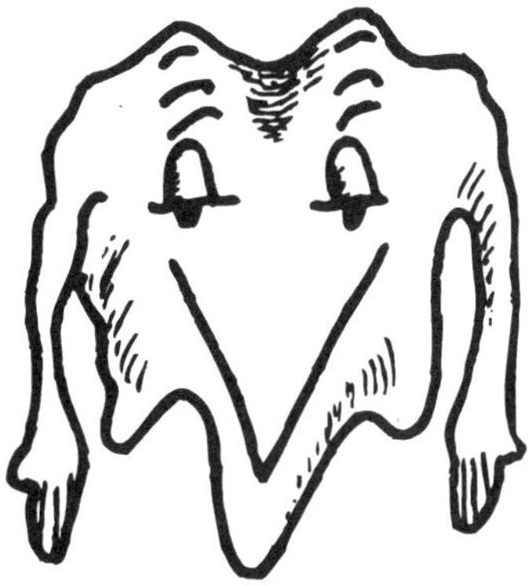

"WHAT'S THE DIFFERENCE?"

Chapter 15

INITIATION RITES—COPING WITH TEASING AND TESTING

CHAPTER SUMMARY

There are many reasons why you may not be welcomed by your supervisor and co-workers in a new job or assignment.

The teasing of the new employee is often nothing more than a way of helping the person become a full-fledged member of the group.

Organizational testing is a deliberate attempt to discover what kind of person you really are and whether you can adjust to certain conditions.

During testing periods you are being watched; the better you react, the sooner it will be over.

RESPONSE TO CHAPTER HIGHLIGHTS

This chapter deals with two kinds of testing. They are:

1. ______________________________

2. ______________________________

Please fill in the missing words:

Teasing, for the most part, is ____________________.

Teasing may get you into trouble if you take it ____________________.

Sometimes, when deep personal testing is involved, it is called a

____________________ conflict.

A frequent cause for deep-seated personal testing is ____________________.

If you react in a negative manner to organizational testing, three things can happen:

1. ______________________________

2. ______________________________

3. ______________________________

Exercise 15 **TEASING AND TESTING**

Listed below are ten "situations." Read each one carefully and then select the proper column (classification) to write out briefly how you would handle it. Suggested answers are provided for the first two situations to help you get started. After you have finished the remaining eight, you might wish to compare your answers with those of the author on the reverse side of this page.

IMPROVEMENTS	PERSONAL TESTING	ORGANIZATIONAL TESTING	PERSONAL TESTING
1. A high school student gets a job in a fast-food operation and is immediately assigned the job of cleaning toilets.		Say thanks and do a good job.	
2. A new employee in a steel mill has her hard-hat hidden the second day by a co-worker.	Go along with the gag.		
3. An employee is asked to serve on a Credit Union committee and is immediately given the job of secretary.			
4. An autocratic boss assigns a minority employee to a task that she is obviously not ready to perform successfully.			
5. A co-worker gives an employee the silent treatment for six months.			
6. An employee is left on a starting job for what seems a long time.			
7. Someone keeps misplacing a new employee's time card.			
8. An employee complains to his supervisor about the behavior of a co-worker.			
9. A supervisor keeps chewing out a new employee in front of others.			
10. A new employee is told that overtime is illegal for the first month an employee works.			

SUGGESTED ANSWERS

3. Organizational testing: Accept assignment with a good attitude.

4. Personal testing (challenging): Go along with it until you have won support of co-workers; then ask for more training.

5. Personal testing (challenging): Ignore it with a smile, don't let it bother you, and keep trying to establish a relationship.

6. Organizational testing: Stay positive as you ask supervisor what you can expect in the future.

7. Personal teasing: Make up a time card of your own. Don't let it bother you.

8. Personal testing (challenging): Confront this employee.

9. Personal testing (challenging): Confront supervisor.

10. Personal teasing: Enjoy the comment and joke back.

CASE STUDY • THE CONSTANT COMPLAINER

Jake was recently transferred to a new department. Everything went well at first, but by the second month he began to feel the effects of the negative comments that flowed, with increasing regularity, from Lee. A few days ago Lee commented: "They want high productivity around here but they buy the cheapest possible equipment and even then they respect the equipment more than employees."

Jake soon discovered that Lee had a long-term reputation as a complainer but never took a complaint of any kind to the supervisor. One day, when Jake's tolerance was somewhat low, Lee started his negative harangue in front of three other co-workers. Jake quickly broke in: "Look, Lee, I know you have seniority around here but if you don't like things the way they are why don't you leave? You don't seem to realize that all your negative talk makes it more difficult for the rest of us." With that, Jake walked away feeling he had done everyone, including the manager, a big favor.

Had he?

Compare your thoughts with those of the author on page 93.

TEST YOURSELF

For each statement below, put a check under true or false.

TRUE	FALSE		
______	______	1.	All working relationships are, in a sense, forced.
______	______	2.	Personal testing is often designed to make you feel welcome.
______	______	3.	Personal teasing (not testing) is often based upon deep-seated prejudice.
______	______	4.	The frequent misplacing of your time card would be a good example of organizational testing.
______	______	5.	A co-worker who seriously bets you won't last thirty days in your new job is demonstrating personal testing (challenging) and not teasing.
______	______	6.	Time will more often take care of organizational testing than personal testing.
______	______	7.	Being on the receiving end of teasing and testing is the price people pay for being the new person on the block.
______	______	8.	An individual should resist any teasing or testing that destroys human dignity.
______	______	9.	Hostility does not manifest itself in pure personal teasing.
______	______	10.	A good supervisor is more apt to be involved in organizational testing than in personal testing.

Turn to the back of the book to check your answers.

TOTAL CORRECT __________

"YES MR. GLUTZ, I'M VERY HAPPY HERE."

Chapter 16

ABSENTEEISM AND HUMAN RELATIONS

CHAPTER SUMMARY

Absenteeism and lateness are more of a problem for management than they used to be.

Management has learned that when an employee or supervisor doesn't show up for work as scheduled, immediate and costly adjustments are necessary.

Chronic lateness by an employee, although not usually as serious or expensive for the organization as absenteeism, is still a problem.

Among other things, excessive absenteeism and lateness will build a credibility gap between you, co-workers, and management.

RESPONSE TO CHAPTER HIGHLIGHTS

The following are frequently cited as causes for the increase in absenteeism:

1. ____________________

2. ____________________

3. ____________________

An employee should not come to work when one of the following conditions exists:

1. ____________________

2. ____________________

3. ____________________

There are two basic reasons why an individual pays a high <u>human-relations</u> price for absenteeism. They are:

1. ____________________

2. ____________________

"The best physicians are Dr. Diet, Dr. Quiet, and Dr. Merryman."

ANON

Exercise 16 **TOLERANCE LEVEL EXERCISE**

The purpose of this exercise is to provide some insight into your own tolerance level for certain behavioral characteristics. If your tolerance level is high, probably co-workers who are frequently absent or late do not hurt their relationship with you very much; if your tolerance level is low, probably they damage their relationship with you. You are to assume the roles of both employee and supervisor so that you can compare your tolerance levels in both positions.

Using the scale of 1 to 10, please indicate your personal tolerance to each of the ten behavioral patterns listed below. If your level is extremely high (it doesn't bother you much), you should write in the number 8, 9, or 10. If your level is extremely low (it really upsets you), write in the number 1, 2, or 3. If you have an average tolerance level, write in a 5.

BEHAVIORAL CHARACTERISTIC OF THE INDIVIDUAL	YOUR TOLERANCE SCORE AS A CO-WORKER	YOUR TOLERANCE SCORE AS A SUPERVISOR
1. Frequently late to work (less than 10 minutes)	_______	_______
2. Frequently late to work (more than 10 minutes)	_______	_______
3. Uses sick leave when not sick	_______	_______
4. Frequently absent without plausible excuse	_______	_______
5. Frequent and extended personal telephone calls	_______	_______
6. Consistently overextends coffee break	_______	_______
7. Spends too much time socializing and discussing personal matters	_______	_______
8. Frequently late at staff meetings (more than 5 minutes)	_______	_______
9. Needs to be reminded to turn in reports on time	_______	_______
10. Frequently takes extended lunch hours	_______	_______
TOTAL SCORE	_______	_______

As you analyze your scores, remember that some of your co-workers or your supervisor might have a lower tolerance level than yours. Your present attitudes toward being late and absent could be having a more damaging effect on your relationships with others than you think.

TEST YOURSELF

For each statement below, put a check under true or false.

TRUE	FALSE		
_____	_____	1.	Management people agree that more and more employees are taking pride in their attendance or on-time records.
_____	_____	2.	In building relationships with co-workers, it is important to take into consideration their tolerance levels.
_____	_____	3.	The absence of an employee usually costs the company money in one way or another.
_____	_____	4.	It is illegal to forward or discuss the absentee record of a former employee with another organization.
_____	_____	5.	It is foolish to save your authorized sick-leave time for real emergencies.
_____	_____	6.	It is better to be ten minutes late than thirty minutes early to work.
_____	_____	7.	When you have a supervisor who has a low tolerance level toward absenteeism, being late will not be so serious.
_____	_____	8.	If your tolerance level toward co-workers' lateness and absenteeism was over 90 on the exercise, you are probably easy to take advantage of in other situations.
_____	_____	9.	Supervisors who have extremely high tolerance levels toward absenteeism and lateness are usually highly respected by both their employees and superiors.
_____	_____	10.	It is easy to repair human relationships damaged by absenteeism.

Turn to the back of the book to check your answers.

TOTAL CORRECT _________

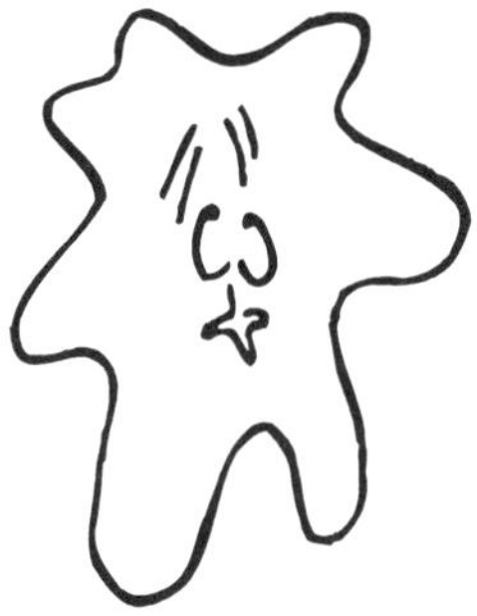

"BUT I WAS REALLY SICK THIS TIME."

Chapter 17

SIX COMMON HUMAN-RELATIONS MISTAKES

CHAPTER SUMMARY

A good way to damage your career progress is to be a poor listener.

Underestimating others can seriously hurt the relationships you may be trying to build with them.

Failure to report or admit mistakes can lead to complicated human-relations problems.

RESPONSE TO CHAPTER HIGHLIGHTS

Give two examples of how failure to listen can cost an organization money.

1. ______________________________

2. ______________________________

Provide an example from the text showing how underestimating others can damage human relations.

____

____

List three primary ways people needlessly victimize themselves.

1. ______________________________

2. ______________________________

3. ______________________________

List the six common mistakes discussed in the chapter.

1. ______________________________

2. ______________________________

3. ______________________________

4. ______________________________

5. ______________________________

6. ______________________________

Exercise 17 **LISTENING SURVEY**

On the following pages are three copies of a listening survey questionnaire that has been field-tested with excellent results. You are encouraged to use it to improve your listening skills. Before you start, however, you should be aware of the following.

1. Most of us are not good listeners, so you may not rate as high as you expect.

2. If you should discover that you are an average listener, or below, do not take it as a personal affront; after all, the idea is to improve your skills from where you are, not from where you think you are.

3. Field testing showed that many people were rated average on the scale; if you rate above average (5 on the scale), this is a compliment to your present listening skills.

In using the Listening Survey Questionnaire, please follow these instructions:

1. Have a minimum of three people complete the questionnaire. You may reproduce as many copies as you wish.

2. Introduce and distribute them only to those individuals who know you well, will take the survey seriously, and will be fair and honest in their responses. Please do not use the questionnaire to restore a relationship with an individual; use it only with those with whom you currently have a very healthy relationship.

3. Give each person an envelope so that they can return the results sealed inside.

4. Give all sealed envelopes to a third person, who should summarize the results for you on a separate piece of paper or a blank photocopy of the questionnaire form (so that you will not know the identity of any single individual).

5. Once you have evaluated the results, make a serious contract with yourself to improve.

"Nothing improves a person's hearing as much as praise."

ANON

LISTENING SURVEY QUESTIONNAIRE

Dear Friend, Fellow-student, Co-worker:

I have made a contract with myself to become a better listener. I am asking you for assistance. Please complete the survey form below, based upon the communications we have had in the past. First, through a comparison with others with whom you have frequent verbal contact, rate me on the listening scale provided. Second, please place a check in any box you think is applicable to me and will help me improve my listening skills. You are also encouraged to write out any suggestions for improvement not covered in the questionnaire.

Once you have finished, place this form in the envelope I have provided and seal it. I will, in turn, give your envelope (along with others) to a third person, who will provide me with a summation sheet. Your anonymity will be protected.

LISTENING SCALE

Outstanding listener (best I know)	10	9	8	7	6	5	4	3	2	1	Extremely poor listener (worst I know)

SUGGESTIONS FOR IMPROVEMENT

You might consider talking less. ________

Refrain from interrupting so much. ________

Be less defensive in communications. ________

Try to stop forming a reply before you hear me out. ________

Relax when you communicate. ________

Slow your mind down so that you won't anticipate what I say before I say it. ________

Be more attentive and send me signals through your eyes so I know you are listening. ________

Improve your concentration. ________

Other suggestions (including compliments)

____

____

____

LISTENING SURVEY QUESTIONNAIRE

Dear Friend, Fellow-student, Co-worker:

I have made a contract with myself to become a better listener. I am asking you for assistance. Please complete the survey form below, based upon the communications we have had in the past. First, through a comparison with others with whom you have frequent verbal contact, rate me on the listening scale provided. Second, please place a check in any box you think is applicable to me and will help me improve my listening skills. You are also encouraged to write out any suggestions for improvement not covered in the questionnaire.

Once you have finished, place this form in the envelope I have provided and seal it. I will, in turn, give your envelope (along with others) to a third person, who will provide me with a summation sheet. Your anonymity will be protected.

LISTENING SCALE

Outstanding listener (best I know)	10	9	8	7	6	5	4	3	2	1	Extremely poor listener (worst I know)

SUGGESTIONS FOR IMPROVEMENT

You might consider talking less. _______

Refrain from interrupting so much. _______

Be less defensive in communications. _______

Try to stop forming a reply before you hear me out. _______

Relax when you communicate. _______

Slow your mind down so that you won't anticipate what I say before I say it. _______

Be more attentive and send me signals through your eyes so I know you are listening. _______

Improve your concentration. _______

Other suggestions (including compliments)

____

____

____

LISTENING SURVEY QUESTIONNAIRE

Dear Friend, Fellow-student, Co-worker:

I have made a contract with myself to become a better listener. I am asking you for assistance. Please complete the survey form below, based upon the communications we have had in the past. First, through a comparison with others with whom you have frequent verbal contact, rate me on the listening scale provided. Second, please place a check in any box you think is applicable to me and will help me improve my listening skills. You are also encouraged to write out any suggestions for improvement not covered in the questionnaire.

Once you have finished, place this form in the envelope I have provided and seal it. I will, in turn, give your envelope (along with others) to a third person, who will provide me with a summation sheet. Your anonymity will be protected.

LISTENING SCALE

Outstanding listener (best I know)	10	9	8	7	6	5	4	3	2	1	Extremely poor listener (worst I know)

SUGGESTIONS FOR IMPROVEMENT

You might consider talking less. _______

Refrain from interrupting so much. _______

Be less defensive in communications. _______

Try to stop forming a reply before you hear me out. _______

Relax when you communicate. _______

Slow your mind down so that you won't anticipate what I say before I say it. _______

Be more attentive and send me signals through your eyes so I know you are listening. _______

Improve your concentration. _______

Other suggestions (including compliments)

____

____

____

TEST YOURSELF

For each statement below, put a check under true or false.

TRUE	FALSE		
______	______	1.	Most people are good listeners.
______	______	2.	People seldom, if ever, know when you are underestimating them.
______	______	3.	It is less dangerous to forget a mistake than to report it.
______	______	4.	You can form a reply in your mind during communications with another without hurting your listening level.
______	______	5.	You will do a better job of listening if you anticipate what people say before they say it.
______	______	6.	Everyone eventually becomes the victim of a damaged relationship.
______	______	7.	If you listen with your eyes (as well as your ears), you are apt to hear better.
______	______	8.	If you hear the sounds, you get the message.
______	______	9.	A substitute phrase for self-victimization is "holding a grudge."
______	______	10.	The more meaningful a relationship, the lower the risk of self-victimization should a conflict occur.

Turn to the back of the book to check your answers.

TOTAL CORRECT ________

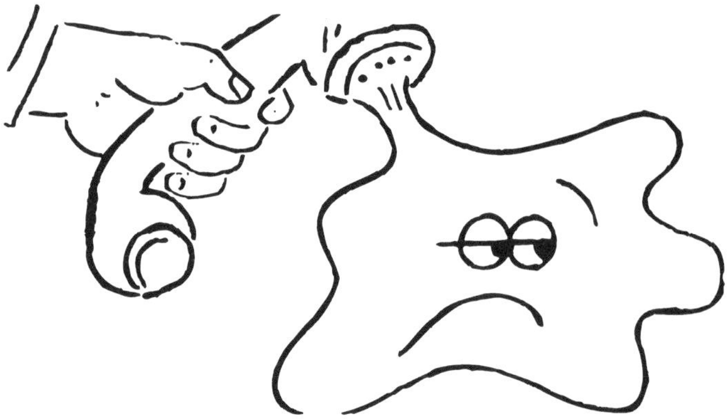

ATTITUDES TRAVEL BY TELEPHONE, TOO. . .

Chapter 18

BUSINESS ETHICS, RUMORS, AND THE CONFIDENCE TRIANGLE

CHAPTER SUMMARY

Ethics is involved in the way people are sometimes treated.

There are certain things you can do to prevent rumors and the rumor mill from hurting your career.

Organization rumors have great influence on the productivity of employees and the general progress of the company.

If you can't say something good about a person, you might be wise not to say anything at all.

RESPONSE TO CHAPTER HIGHLIGHTS

Summarize six things you can do to safeguard your career against unfounded rumors.

1. ______________________________

2. ______________________________

3. ______________________________

4. ______________________________

5. ______________________________

6. ______________________________

Sketch a "confidence triangle" below and explain how it works.

____

____

____

____

____

Name three attitudes that can improve your ethical behavior.

1. ______________________________

2. ______________________________

3. ______________________________

Exercise 18 **THE CONFIDENCE TRIANGLE EXERCISE**

One of the messages of Chapter 18 is that if you can't say something good about another person, don't say anything. In short, bad-mouthing others is dangerous. This exercise presents five situations and then lists various possible outcomes. Please place a check in the blank after those possible outcomes that you feel might actually happen. The purpose of the project is to make you more aware of the dangers of casual conversations where confidence is implied.

SITUATION	POSSIBLE OUTCOMES	
May is having lunch with Sue. Sue says, "just between you and me, I think that our supervisor is being unfair to you." May replies, "Don't worry about it. I am going to get her job if it's the last thing I ever do."	Sue might carry May's threat back to the supervisor.	______
	May might lose Sue's friendship.	______
	May might be motivated into unethical behavior to get the supervisor's job. This could backfire.	______
	Sue might offer to pay for the lunch.	______
John's supervisor calls him into his office and says, "I know that you are having trouble with your assistant, but don't worry about it because he is on his way out." John, returning to his department, comments to a co-worker, "Relax, my assistant is being given the shaft by the boss."	The supervisor might lose his or her job instead of the assistant.	______
	The co-worker might carry the word to the assistant and get John in trouble.	______
	John will have more respect for the supervisor.	______
	The co-worker will like John better.	______
	John will get a raise.	______
Mary is having coffee with her close friend Ralph, who is a supervisor in another department. Mary says, "Ralph, my supervisor is a stinker. If he isn't making a play for me, it is one of the other women."	Ralph may tell Mary's supervisor that Mary is jealous of the attention he is paying to others.	______
	Ralph may tell Mary's supervisor to cool it.	______
	Ralph may report Mary's supervisor to upper management.	______
	Ralph may think less of Mary.	______
	Ralph may say nothing.	______

SITUATION	POSSIBLE OUTCOMES	
Martha and Marge are having lunch in the company cafeteria. Martha says, "Tell me, how are you getting along with that new employee Sylvia? Frankly, I think she is the best new worker we have had around here in years." Marge replies, "I couldn't agree more."	Marge may pay Sylvia a compliment by communicating Martha's comments.	_____
	Martha may pay Sylvia a compliment by communicating Marge's comments.	_____
	Martha and Marge may get along better in the future.	_____
	Sylvia may try even harder to win acceptance of others.	_____
Harry is a supervisor competing with Dolores for a mid-management job. While having coffee with Randy from another department, Harry says, "I guess I will have to wait longer for my promotion than I thought. I know Dolores is going to win because she is the right sex and comes from a minority culture. I'm going to polish up my resumé and scramble to another company."	Randy may feel Harry is bigoted and fight against his progress in the future.	_____
	Harry's comments might kill his chance for this promotion.	_____
	Randy might spread the word that Harry is so unhappy that he has found another job.	_____
	Randy could feel sorry for Harry and do more to help him.	_____
	Randy may relate the conversation to Dolores, who, in turn, will intensify her efforts to win the promotion.	_____
	Dolores, upon hearing that Randy is leaving, may slow down her efforts to get the promotion, thus letting Harry get the edge.	_____
	Dolores may decide to "get" Harry.	_____
	Harry may live to regret his comments.	_____
	None of the above will happen.	_____

"The only thing to do with good advice is to pass it on. It is never of any use to oneself."

Oscar Wilde

TEST YOURSELF

For each statement below, put a check under true or false.

TRUE	FALSE		
______	______	1.	Most human-relations problems are self-created.
______	______	2.	A good way to improve the relationship between you and the person to whom you are talking is to bad-mouth others.
______	______	3.	Business ethics is not an appropriate subject in a human relations text.
______	______	4.	Few comments shared with a confidant are passed on to others.
______	______	5.	In most organizations it is the grapevine that generates rumors.
______	______	6.	Divulging confidential corporate information is considered to be unethical.
______	______	7.	Chances are you will not find a rumor mill where you work.
______	______	8.	You should not permit information received via the grapevine to disturb you personally because it could hurt your productivity and eventually your career.
______	______	9.	One person can often break the circuit in a typical grapevine.
______	______	10.	Normally, management does not know whether a rumor mill or a grapevine exists.

Turn to the back of the book to check your answers.

TOTAL CORRECT _________

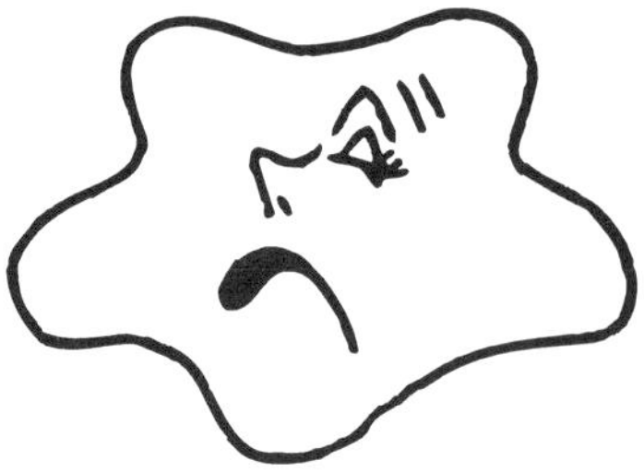

"LOOK AT ALL THAT WORK SHE'S TURNING OUT . . ."

Chapter 19

GOAL SETTING AND ATTITUDE

CHAPTER SUMMARY

It is generally accepted that there is a connection between goals and attitude. Those with realistic goals maintain, on the average, more positive attitudes.

Goals are more frequently reached when they are accompanied with personal rewards when progress is made.

For both career and lifestyle success, it is wise to design a "goal pattern" that meets your individual needs.

RESPONSE TO CHAPTER HIGHLIGHTS

In a single sentence, write down what insights you gained from the following individuals around which vignettes were written. When finished, compare your insights to those printed at the bottom of the page.

Adelle ______________________________

____

Drake ______________________________

____

Camcron ______________________________

____

Janette ______________________________

Adelle: Sometimes having a personal goal motivates one to do better in a non-related area.

Drake: Some people mistakenly ignore the need for "fun" or leisure goals.

Cameron: Most people need a balance between career, family, and leisure goals.

Janette: Everyone needs some free time just for themselves.

Exercise 19 **DESIGNING A MASTER GOAL PATTERN**

Using the outline below, designate your current goals and the rewards you have attached to them. If you do not have a goal or reward for a category, please add one. Keep in mind that we are dealing with career, lifestyle, family, and pleasure goals.

GOALS	REWARDS

Daily Goals.

______________________ ______________________

______________________ ______________________

Weekly Goals.

______________________ ______________________

______________________ ______________________

Monthly Goals.

______________________ ______________________

______________________ ______________________

Annual Goals.

______________________ ______________________

______________________ ______________________

Life Goals.

______________________ ______________________

______________________ ______________________

TEST YOURSELF

For each statement below, put a check under true or false.

TRUE	FALSE		
______	______	1.	The primary beneficiary of having goals is your attitude.
______	______	2.	Most goal-oriented people do not have time for fun activities so they become negative.
______	______	3.	When you are expecting to reach a goal you are more apt to reach it.
______	______	4.	Giving yourself rewards when you make progress toward goals gives your attitude a boost.
______	______	5.	Most people are blind to their need to have some quality time for themselves.
______	______	6.	Management experts claim it is a good idea to write down daily and weekly work goals.
______	______	7.	Designing a master goal pattern can help you keep a more balanced life.
______	______	8.	Students do not need goals as much as full-time career people.
______	______	9.	Setting goals almost always leads to frustration and disappointment.
______	______	10.	The only goals worth having are those that are self-motivating.

Turn to the back of the book to check your answers.

TOTAL CORRECT ________

Chapter 20

TWO ROUTES TO THE TOP

CHAPTER SUMMARY

There are two basic ways in which employees can build their careers and reach upper-management levels. One is to stay with one organization; the other is to move from one organization to another.

There are advantages and disadvantages to both routes.

Any one who works for someone else can benefit from a Plan B.

RESPONSE TO CHAPTER HIGHLIGHTS

Please list the advantages of joining a PFW organization.

1. ____________________

2. ____________________

3. ____________________

Please list the advantages of taking the "zigzag" route.

1. ____________________

2. ____________________

3. ____________________

Many observers claim that scramblers are more highly motivated than stabilizers. Do you agree? If so, state reasons why you feel this is true. If you feel that stabilizers are equally motivated (or more highly motivated) build your case in that direction.

____

Name five factors you would take into consideration in evaluating a work environment for yourself.

1. ____________________

2. ____________________

3. ____________________

4. ____________________

5. ____________________

Exercise 20 **SCRAMBLER VS. STABILIZER SCALE**

Chapter 20 discusses the advantages and disadvantages of building a career with one large organization versus taking the zigzag route, or moving from one firm to another. This exercise may give you some additional insight into your behavioral characteristics, which can, in turn, lead you to a better decision.

Please circle the number that indicates where you fall in the scale of 1 to 10.

I need a great deal of freedom. Rules and regulations annoy me.	10	9	8	7	6	5	4	3	2	1	I can easily adhere to rules and regulations without becoming hostile.
I like to take risks even if I get into confrontations with management.	10	9	8	7	6	5	4	3	2	1	I hate risks and I want to avoid any confrontations with management.
Two or three years is long enough to stay with any organization.	10	9	8	7	6	5	4	3	2	1	I like the idea of spending my entire career with the same organization.
I do not have enough patience to succeed inside a large organization.	10	9	8	7	6	5	4	3	2	1	I have all the patience necessary to be successful in a large organization.
If I can't have both, I would rather have a high salary and smaller benefits.	10	9	8	7	6	5	4	3	2	1	I would rather have a lower salary and a much better benefit package.
I hate plateau periods and will fight to overcome them.	10	9	8	7	6	5	4	3	2	1	I can learn to live gracefully through long plateau periods.
I love to beat the system.	10	9	8	7	6	5	4	3	2	1	I never try to beat the system.
I have always considered myself to be something of a rebel.	10	9	8	7	6	5	4	3	2	1	My characteristic is to adjust rather than fight.

I'll move anywhere in the United States to get a better job at a higher salary.	10 9 8 7 6 5 4 3 2 1	I would turn down a better job at a much higher salary to stay where I am.
I get tense when people try to box me in or stifle my creativity.	10 9 8 7 6 5 4 3 2 1	I can remain calm when bureaucratic restrictions are imposed.

TOTAL SCORE ___________

If you rated yourself 60 or above, you may be receiving a signal that you should be a scrambler. If you rated yourself above 80, the signal is much stronger. Perhaps you would be uncomfortable in a big organization with a highly structured environment. You might find yourself fighting the restrictions and hurting your career progress. In other words, the zigzag route to the top could make more sense for you than joining and staying with a single, promotion-from-within organization for your entire career.

If you rated yourself under 40, you may be getting a signal that you should be a stabilizer. A slower, more secure upward mobility pattern might be better for you. This means that you might be able to handle problems and progress faster inside a conservative firm.

If you rated yourself between 40 and 60, you are not receiving a clear signal either way. You might find it difficult to handle a high-risk, fast-moving firm; on the other hand, a very conservative firm might cause you to be impatient. The signal might mean that you should stay clear of both a highly aggressive and a highly conservative company—something in the middle could be the best working environment for you.

There are many indications that a growing number of ambitious people are opting for the zigzag route these days. Statistics also show that movement of employees from one company to another is on the increase—especially at upper levels.

It is also important to keep in mind that more and more large organizations are going through reorganizations which have the tendency to make scramblers out of stabilizers whether they want to be or not.

INSIGHT

It is easy to separate those with positive and negative attitudes when they go on vacations. The positive workers are missed and welcomed back. The negative ones give those remaining at work a much needed vacation. The point, of course, is that your positive attitude is priceless to you—it is also greatly valued by others!

TEST YOURSELF

For each statement below, put a check under true or false.

TRUE	FALSE		
______	______	1.	Stabilizers do not need a Plan B.
______	______	2.	A Plan B means switching to a different career area.
______	______	3.	The zigzag route is more risky.
______	______	4.	Ambitious people with high tolerance levels might find it best to build a career inside a large organization that believes in the PFW policy.
______	______	5.	PFW doesn't mean as much as it used to.
______	______	6.	An applicant should attempt to discover the existence or non-existence of a PFW policy during the interview process.
______	______	7.	The zigzag route provides more security and less moving from one geographical area to another.
______	______	8.	Economic conditions (mergers–reorganizations) are forcing some organizations to abandon their PFW policies.
______	______	9.	A Plan B often helps an employee do a better job with his or her Plan A.
______	______	10.	The more competitive and aggressive an individual is, the more she or he should consider building a career by moving from one organization to another whenever there is an advantage in doing so.

Turn to the back of the book to check your answers.

TOTAL CORRECT __________

"THINGS SURE MOVE SLOW AROUND HERE."

Chapter 21

KEEPING A POSITIVE ATTITUDE THROUGH PLATEAU PERIODS AND REORGANIZATIONS

CHAPTER SUMMARY

Plateau or waiting periods are normal in all organizations.

There are, however, many things the employee can do to either shorten them or convert them into learning and preparation periods.

The most important thing to remember is that if one's attitude begins to show in a negative manner during these periods (with a subsequent drop in personal productivity), then plateau periods can become longer instead of shorter.

RESPONSE TO CHAPTER HIGHLIGHTS

Please write out five questions you might ask yourself to help you do a better job of surviving a plateau period.

1. ______________________________

2. ______________________________

3. ______________________________

4. ______________________________

5. ______________________________

Fill in the missing words in these sentences.

It is difficult to wear a ______________ ______________.

A long plateau period can destroy one's ______________.

Most executives have lived through ______________ periods.

Most executives believe in promotion by ______________.

Listed below are five things you might do to prepare yourself should your organization go through a restructuring and layoff program. Check those you plan to do.

- ☐ Keep my resume updated.
- ☐ Maintain better contact with potential employers.
- ☐ Maintain a network of people who could help me relocate.
- ☐ Keep learning both on-the-job and at seminars.
- ☐ Stay flexible regarding career objectives and geographical locations.

Exercise 21 THINGS TO DO TO SHORTEN A LENGTHY PLATEAU PERIOD

Most ambitious employees eventually find themselves on a plateau where they must put on their "patience suits" until something breaks in their favor. The purpose of this exercise is to help you select appropriate steps to shorten these periods or at least prevent them from hurting your attitude.

Listed below are twenty action steps you could take in such a situation. If you have never been employed, this exercise can still be of value to you. You are asked to select only those steps that are appropriate to your style and personality—steps you would actually take. Please make a check for each possible step.

ACTION STEPS	APPROPRIATE FOR ME	NOT APPROPRIATE FOR ME
1. Become more assertive.	_______	_______
2. Start looking for another job and let your organization know you are doing so.	_______	_______
3. Let the word out that you are looking for another job but don't bother to do it.	_______	_______
4. Play some politics like the others and don't worry about ethics.	_______	_______
5. Work harder. Become more motivated. Live closer to your potential. Don't give up.	_______	_______
6. Spend more time creating and maintaining good human relations at all levels. Improve skills in this area.	_______	_______
7. Keep your motivation up by taking a night course appropriate to your career goals.	_______	_______
8. Submit a well-researched suggestion to management to gain recognition.	_______	_______
9. Remain patient and effective; let others become aggressive and overplay their hands.	_______	_______
10. Talk to people who have lived through such periods and follow their advice.	_______	_______
11. Ask someone in personnel to help you update your resumé.	_______	_______
12. Get a job moonlighting to earn more money so that some of the pressure on you will be dissipated.	_______	_______
13. Take your supervisor to lunch.	_______	_______

(Continue on next page.)

ACTION STEPS	APPROPRIATE FOR ME	NOT APPROPRIATE FOR ME
14. Start doing irregular things (not your normal behavior) that defy traditional protocol so that you can gain more attention.	______	______
15. Create some modest waves by doing a few things that need to be done without asking permission to do them.	______	______
16. Ask for a raise in pay.	______	______
17. Capitalize on the situation by deliberately projecting a "patient" image, but do everything possible to push yourself.	______	______
18. Ask for a transfer.	______	______
19. Talk to your supervisor's superior.	______	______
20. Resign.	______	______
TOTAL	______	______

If you checked eight or more in the "appropriate for me" column, chances are you could shorten any plateau period. Of course, it would depend to some extent on the skill you used in taking the steps. If you checked five or fewer, your chance of success would be less.

It should be obvious that certain of the above steps could do more harm than good. But without some action on your part, management could ignore you or promote someone ahead of you because they feel you are a "nice patient person" and will not resign, no matter what happens.

INSIGHT

A sensitive outsider can usually tell when a work environment is comfortable, efficient, and productive by observing the attitudes of workers. There is more laughter. Employees are more tolerant of each other. Work is viewed more as a rewarding team effort than a series of boring tasks. But make no mistake! A single negative attitude can start turning a harmonious atmosphere sour.

TEST YOURSELF

For each statement below, put a check under true or false.

TRUE	FALSE		
______	______	1.	Assertive people have more success in shortening or eliminating plateau periods.
______	______	2.	When you find yourself on a plateau in a large organization, the only thing to do is be patient and wait it out.
______	______	3.	Some employees feel they are on a plateau when they still have much to learn.
______	______	4.	If organizations really wanted to, they could eliminate plateau periods.
______	______	5.	Doing something spectacular that doesn't backfire can shorten a plateau period.
______	______	6.	Management can eliminate all the pressure points an employee stuck on a plateau period faces.
______	______	7.	The most dangerous possibility in living through a plateau period is that one's attitude might turn negative, causing management to promote someone else.
______	______	8.	Knowing more about plateau periods can help one live through them gracefully.
______	______	9.	Asking for a horizontal transfer during a plateau period is nothing but a "copout."
______	______	10.	Patience is something one learns in college.

Turn to the back of the book to check your answers.

TOTAL CORRECT __________

"ANOTHER REORGANIZATION."

Chapter 22

WHEN YOU ARE TEMPTED TO SCRAMBLE

CHAPTER SUMMARY

As a general rule, you should resign when you have been unhappy and unproductive for a considerable period of time.

Surveys and statistics show, however, that most resignations are based primarily upon personality conflicts and human problems.

If you lose your job because of a layoff or cutback, it could be discouraging. If, however, you lose your positive attitude along with the job, you are a double loser. Maintain a positive attitude and go out and find yourself a more rewarding position.

RESPONSE TO CHAPTER HIGHLIGHTS

Please list three questions you would ask yourself when considering a resignation. The text lists seven.

1. ______________________________

2. ______________________________

3. ______________________________

Please list five tips you would give to a friend on how to resign a job gracefully. The text lists nine.

1. ______________________________

2. ______________________________

3. ______________________________

4. ______________________________

5. ______________________________

Name four ways you would protect your positive attitude during a change of ownership or major restructuring where you work.

1. ______________________________

2. ______________________________

3. ______________________________

4. ______________________________

Exercise 22 **PLAN B EXERCISE**

A Plan B is a carefully researched and designed strategy to provide a new job immediately should your present one disappear or lose its luster. A Plan B should be considered a reserve program that will match or be superior to your present job or Plan A. This exercise is designed to help you decide whether or not you initiate a Plan B. Read both statements carefully, then circle the number most appropriate in your case. A 10 indicates you have an extremely high desire to have a Plan B. A 1 indicates you have no interest.

	HIGH									LOW	
I want to prepare now for possible winds of change.	10	9	8	7	6	5	4	3	2	1	I'll face change when it happens.
I view a Plan B as a most important insurance policy.	10	9	8	7	6	5	4	3	2	1	I view Plan B as a waste of time.
Having a Plan B will help me feel better about my Plan A.	10	9	8	7	6	5	4	3	2	1	Nothing can make me feel better about my Plan A.
I agree a Plan B will help me get a new job if needed.	10	9	8	7	6	5	4	3	2	1	It is best to wait until the last minute.
I understand that a Plan B may require I upgrade my skills.	10	9	8	7	6	5	4	3	2	1	I'm sticking with my skills as they exist.
A Plan B can help one get a promotion with his/her present firm.	10	9	8	7	6	5	4	3	2	1	Preparing a Plan B can get you fired.
Both scramblers and stabilizers need to develop a Plan B.	10	9	8	7	6	5	4	3	2	1	Advance planning leads to severe disappointment.
I agree a Plan B should be a written strategy including an updated resumé, etc.	10	9	8	7	6	5	4	3	2	1	The only Plan B worth the effort is an idea in your mind.
I see the need for a Plan B and will start one as soon as I have landed a good Plan A.	10	9	8	7	6	5	4	3	2	1	Sorry, I just don't see the need.
A Plan B is designed to help one remain professional in his or her specialty.	10	9	8	7	6	5	4	3	2	1	I'm not worried about being a professional. All I want is a job.

TOTAL _______

If you rated yourself 80 or above, you have an excellent attitude toward having a formal Plan B. A score between 60 and 80 indicates enough interest to start one. A score under 60 is a signal that the individual is not interested at this point in his or her life.

TEST YOURSELF

For each statement below, put a check under true or false.

TRUE	FALSE		
______	______	1.	Most resignations are irrevocable.
______	______	2.	You would be wise not to resign until after you have discussed the problem with your supervisor or someone in the Human Resource department.
______	______	3.	Resigning because of personality conflict is not a good way to build a lifelong career.
______	______	4.	It does not hurt your reputation if you are terminated because of a layoff, cutback, or furlough situation.
______	______	5.	Always resign a position in such a manner that you feel free to seek reemployment with the same organization at a later date.
______	______	6.	It is still important to give ample notice.
______	______	7.	Never accept a job until you have compared it to two others.
______	______	8.	Having a Plan B helps one remain positive during periods of dramatic organizational change.
______	______	9.	In the long run, a good learning environment can pay off better than a high initial salary.
______	______	10.	All of the answers to the above statements should be marked true.

Turn to the back of the book to check your answers.

TOTAL CORRECT ________

"THINGS ALWAYS LOOK BETTER ELSEWHERE."

Chapter 23

ATTITUDE RENEWAL

CHAPTER SUMMARY

A positive attitude can help one do better at handling job stress. Attitude renewal or restoration is a daily, weekly, and sometimes a "major overhaul" process.

Like maintaining an automobile, no one can stay out of an "attitude repair" indefinitely.

An "attitudinal rut" is when an individual's focus is permanently skewed to the negative side of his or her perception.

Attitude renewal starts with self-appraisal. This is true because you can fall into a "rut" without knowing it and people can send you signals that YOUR ATTITUDE IS SHOWING—but you may not receive them.

RESPONSE TO CHAPTER HIGHLIGHTS

In the spaces below, list the five ATTITUDE ADJUSTMENT TECHNIQUES according to your own personal preferences. Please explain why you prefer your first two choices over the others.

1. ______________________________ (Write out below why this was

your first choice.) ______________________________

____

____

____

2. ______________________________ (Write out below why this was

your second choice.) ______________________________

____

____

____

3. ______________________________

4. ______________________________

5. ______________________________

"Blessed are those who can give without remembering, and take without forgetting."

ELIZABETH BIBESCO

Exercise 23 **ATTITUDE ADJUSTMENT APPLICATION EXERCISE**

It is one thing to learn—it is another thing to use. But when you actually use a technique you not only will remember it longer, the chances are better that you will continue to use it in other situations. With this in mind, write out how you intend to use the following techniques to improve your attitude. When possible, deal with a current problem you may be facing.

THE FLIPSIDE TECHNIQUE: (Do you have a current problem you can turn around so you can laugh at it a little?)

PLAY YOUR WINNERS TECHNIQUE: (How about rewarding yourself with one of your WINNERS tonight so that your attitude will be more positive tomorrow?)

GIVE YOUR POSITIVE ATTITUDE AWAY TECHNIQUE: (Why not be extra nice to somebody today whom you normally ignore?)

LOOK BETTER TO YOURSELF TECHNIQUE: (How about a change in your hairstyle?)

ACCEPT THE PHYSICAL CONNECTION TECHNIQUE: (Could you benefit from a special workout today?)

TEST YOURSELF

For each statement below, put a check under true or false.

TRUE	FALSE		
_____	_____	1.	Some job stress is self-imposed.
_____	_____	2.	A positive attitude can be an antidote to job stress.
_____	_____	3.	It is easy to make the transition from being negative at work to positive at home.
_____	_____	4.	A good "funny focus" can get you out of the problem into the solution.
_____	_____	5.	If you are a religious person, praying is a way to PLAY YOUR WINNERS.
_____	_____	6.	It is better to give a co-worker a piece of your positive attitude than your mind.
_____	_____	7.	An inferiority complex is when you look better to others than you do to yourself.
_____	_____	8.	It is absurd to call a health club an ATTITUDE ADJUSTMENT FACTORY.
_____	_____	9.	The easier it is to give your positive attitude away, the more it does for you.
_____	_____	10.	It is better to look good to others than to yourself.

Turn to the back of the book to check your answers.

TOTAL CORRECT _________

"MY ATTITUDE IS OVER ADJUSTED."

Chapter 24

SHOULD YOU BECOME A MANAGER OR A LEADER?

CHAPTER SUMMARY

Deciding whether or not to be a supervisor deserves careful analysis of many factors.

Everything you have learned about human relations as an employee will help you even more should you become a supervisor.

The more you put your new human-relations skills into practice the more self-confident you will become.

RESPONSE TO CHAPTER HIGHLIGHTS

List six factors from the book that deserve careful consideration when an individual is thinking about preparing to become a supervisor.

1. ____________________

2. ____________________

3. ____________________

4. ____________________

5. ____________________

6. ____________________

It is generally accepted that completing a course in human relations is excellent preparation for becoming a supervisor. Listed below are ten skill preparation areas covered in YOUR ATTITUDE IS SHOWING. Check the three that you feel would serve you best as a new supervisor.

- ☐ Knowing how to stay positive under pressure.
- ☐ Understanding the nature of working relationships.
- ☐ The Mutual Reward Theory.
- ☐ How to release your frustrations harmlessly.
- ☐ Knowing how to restore injured relationships.
- ☐ Knowledge of rumor mills and grapevines.
- ☐ Knowing when to scramble.
- ☐ Attitude toward renewal techniques.
- ☐ Being skillful at communication.
- ☐ Being sensitive to the needs of others.

Exercise 24 **SUPERVISOR ANALYSIS SCALE**

If you have not had the opportunity to think about whether or not you would like to become a supervisor, this scale should help. Circle the number that indicates where you fall in the scale from 1 to 10. After you have finished, total your scores in the space provided.

I can develop the confidence to become an outstanding supervisor.	10	9	8	7	6	5	4	3	2	1	I could never be even an average supervisor.
I have the capacity to build and maintain productive relationships with workers under my supervision.	10	9	8	7	6	5	4	3	2	1	I'm a loner. I do not want the responsibility of building and maintaining relationships with others.
It does not bother me that supervisors are more vulnerable and subject to criticism.	10	9	8	7	6	5	4	3	2	1	I could not handle the criticism that most supervisors receive.
I can develop the skill of motivating others.	10	9	8	7	6	5	4	3	2	1	I could never develop the skill of motivating.
I can be patient, fair, consistent, and understanding with others.	10	9	8	7	6	5	4	3	2	1	I have no patience and understanding for others, and could not develop it.
I could learn to be good at disciplining those under me—even to the point of terminating a worker after repeated violations.	10	9	8	7	6	5	4	3	2	1	It would tear me up to discipline a worker under my supervision, I'm much too kind and sensitive.
I can make tough decisions of all kinds.	10	9	8	7	6	5	4	3	2	1	I do not want decision-making responsibilities.
It would not bother me to isolate myself from those I would supervise.	10	9	8	7	6	5	4	3	2	1	I have a great need to be liked; I want to be one of the gang and enjoy working.
I would make an outstanding member of a management team.	10	9	8	7	6	5	4	3	2	1	I hate staff meetings and would be a weak or hostile member of a management team.
My human-relations training will make me a superior supervisor—better than anyone I have worked under.	10	9	8	7	6	5	4	3	2	1	Despite my human-relations training, my potential as a supervisor is so low it is not worth developing.

TOTAL SCORE ________

If you scored 80 or above, it would appear that you have the potential to become an excellent supervisor. If you scored between 50 and 80, you may need to gain more confidence, but you seem to have the potential to become a highly successful leader. If you rated yourself under 50, you probably are not ready for a supervisory role at this stage of your life.

TEST YOURSELF

For each statement below, put a check under true or false.

TRUE	FALSE		
____	____	1.	Employees who practice good human relations become supervisors sooner.
____	____	2.	Few specific human-relations skills you learn as an employee are usable if you become a supervisor.
____	____	3.	An individual who has both technical and human-relations skills is said to have a double competency.
____	____	4.	Improving one's human-relations skills does little to increase one's self-confidence.
____	____	5.	It is easier to become a supervisor today because management training is less demanding.
____	____	6.	Many excellent employees make poor supervisors because they are unable to correct the bad behavior of those who work for them.
____	____	7.	An example of a hard decision would be having to release a good, loyal employee because of a layoff beyond your control.
____	____	8.	Supervisors do not get as much satisfaction from their jobs as employees.
____	____	9.	Ambitious people who like more responsibility, enjoy decision making, and are sensitive to needs of others should seriously consider becoming a supervisor.
____	____	10.	Becoming a supervisor will force you to live closer to your potential.

Turn to the back of the book to check your answers.

TOTAL CORRECT ________

"LET HIM SWEAT! HE'S GETTING PAID FOR IT. . ."

CASE STUDY • PHIL AND JUDY

Phil feels that his future depends more on keeping up with the new technology than on human relations. He is currently taking an advanced course in computer programming and is vice-president of the local chapter of AISP (Association of Information Systems Professionals). He prides himself on knowing as much as possible about the machines he operates. For example, when the maintenance person comes to the office, he is full of technical questions. Phil is popular in the office because he is always willing to help those who are still confused over the rapid changes in the computer system. His co-workers feel that when more sophisticated equipment arrives, Phil will be able and willing to help them.

Judy is also interested in computers, but her main focus is on human relations and management. Instead of taking an advanced course in computer technology, she is taking a course in how to become a good office manager. Judy feels that if she can keep up with the average worker on the technical side, but pass everyone up on the management skills side that she will eventually be promoted. Judy uses her personality power whenever an opportunity presents itself. She is not afraid to bend a few rules. She takes chances.

Which employee do you feel has the greatest chance for success in an automated office? Do you identify more with Phil or Judy? Write out your answer in the space below. As you do this, keep in mind that in most organizations there are advanced positions both in management and technical roles.

Match your thoughts with those of the author by turning to page 93.

"The means to gain happiness is to throw out from oneself like a spider in all directions an adhesive web of love, and catch in it all that comes."

LEO TOLSTOY

THE TAKER • page 8

Action should always be taken when the behavior of one individual begins to hurt the productivity of the group. In this case, the manager should initiate a series of one-on-one conferences with Maureen to discover the reason for her problem. Does she have a skill deficiency she is covering up or is she in fact intimidated by the machine? A positive attitude is a beautiful thing, but it is not enough alone. The right kind of training on the equipment could solve the problem. If not, reassignment may be in order.

THE LONER • page 17

As long as Mrs. Grace is a high producer herself and does not irritate others to the point that it interferes with their productivity, she should be left alone. Her co-workers, hopefully, will come to realize that her high productivity takes some of the pressure away from them and that Mrs. Grace needs (and is entitled to) her privacy. Sometimes shy or withdrawn employees are perceived by co-workers as hostile or "superior." As long as this doesn't happen, no direct action is necessary. If, however, Mrs. Grace's reading and letter writing begin to take precedence over her office assignments, immediate action should be taken.

MR. OVERTIME • page 40

First of all, Mrs. Adams should talk over her child-care situation with her manager. In doing so, she should stress that she does not want special treatment, just consistency. She should then explain that because the job is so ideal for her she is willing to work harder during the time she is in the office. Mrs. Adams should then ask if it is possible for her to be assigned work that she could finish up the following day so that her productivity in the morning hours would be even higher. Her manager will probably agree. Most managers are anxious to demonstrate their flexibility when it will result in making them look better to their superiors.

THE UNDISCIPLINED WORKER • page 45

Sara might consider taking Cassie out for dinner to talk about the matter before it is too late. Sara should not pry into Cassie's personal life but offer practical suggestions that will help her learn to keep her two worlds separate. It might help to jot down some of the suggestions on a piece of paper. In any case, Sara should point out to Cassie that, from her own experience, she knows that those who cannot keep their work and play worlds separate eventually lose the support of co-workers and management. At that point, resignation (voluntary or otherwise) is often the only solution.

THE CONSTANT COMPLAINER • page 56

Jake did the right thing. Silence is often interpreted to be consent or agreement, and Jake has an obligation to protect his own positive attitude. The fact that Lee had been in the department longer than Jake is irrelevant. Although such outspoken comments are disturbing temporarily, they often "clear the air." Jake is demonstrating his leadership potential, and it could enhance his opportunity to become a manager. It could also earn him the respect of his co-workers.

PHIL AND JUDY • page 91

The author admires Phil's technical competence and willingness to help others maintain their technical skills, but he may be shortsighted in not "balancing" things out with more human relations training. Judy, on the other hand, may be moving too far in the other direction. Those who gain upward mobility in highly technical organizations need to achieve the best possible balance in both directions.

ANSWERS TO TRUE/FALSE QUESTIONS

Chapter 1

1. F
2. F
3. T
4. T
5. F
6. T
7. T
8. T
9. T
10. T

Chapter 2

1. T
2. F
3. F
4. T
5. F
6. F
7. F
8. T
9. T
10. F

Chapter 3

1. T
2. F
3. F
4. T
5. T
6. T
7. F
8. T
9. T
10. T

Chapter 4

1. T
2. T
3. F
4. F
5. T
6. T
7. T
8. T
9. T
10. T

Chapter 5

1. T
2. F
3. F
4. F
5. T
6. F
7. F
8. T
9. T
10. F

Chapter 6

1. F
2. T
3. T
4. F
5. F
6. F
7. T
8. T
9. T
10. F

Chapter 7

1. F
2. T
3. F
4. F
5. T
6. F
7. F
8. F
9. T
10. F

Chapter 8

1. T
2. F
3. T
4. T
5. T
6. T
7. F
8. T
9. F
10. T

Chapter 9

1. T
2. T
3. T
4. T
5. T
6. T
7. T
8. T
9. T
10. T

Chapter 10

1. T
2. F
3. T
4. T
5. F
6. T
7. T
8. F
9. F
10. F

ANSWERS TO TRUE/FALSE QUESTIONS

Chapter 11

1. F
2. T
3. T
4. T
5. T
6. T
7. F
8. T
9. T
10. T

Chapter 12

1. T
2. F
3. F
4. T
5. T
6. T
7. F
8. F
9. F
10. T

Chapter 13

1. T
2. F
3. T
4. T
5. T
6. F
7. F
8. T
9. T
10. F

Chapter 14

1. T
2. T
3. T
4. T
5. T
6. T
7. T
8. F
9. T
10. T

Chapter 15

1. T
2. F
3. F
4. F
5. T
6. T
7. T
8. T
9. T
10. T

Chapter 16

1. F
2. T
3. T
4. F
5. F
6. F
7. F
8. T
9. F
10. F

Chapter 17

1. F
2. F
3. F
4. F
5. F
6. T
7. T
8. F
9. T
10. F

Chapter 18

1. T
2. F
3. F
4. F
5. F
6. T
7. F
8. T
9. T
10. F

Chapter 19

1. T
2. F
3. T
4. T
5. F
6. T
7. T
8. F
9. F
10. T

Chapter 20

1. F
2. F
3. T
4. F
5. T
6. T
7. F
8. T
9. T
10. T

ANSWERS TO TRUE/FALSE QUESTIONS

Chapter 21

1. T
2. F
3. T
4. F
5. T
6. F
7. T
8. T
9. F
10. F

Chapter 22

1. T
2. T
3. T
4. T
5. T
6. T
7. T
8. T
9. T
10. T

Chapter 23

1. T
2. T
3. F
4. T
5. T
6. T
7. T
8. F
9. F
10. F

Chapter 24

1. T
2. F
3. T
4. F
5. F
6. T
7. T
8. F
9. T
10. T